CHRISTIANS IN
HELL

IS YOUR FAITH MERELY FALSE HOPE?

CHRISTIANS IN
HELL

DANIEL P. FRANKLIN

TATE PUBLISHING & Enterprises

Published by Tate Publishing & Enterprises, LLC
127 E. Trade Center Terrace | Mustang, Oklahoma 73064 USA
1.888.361.9473 | www.tatepublishing.com

Tate Publishing is committed to excellence in the publishing industry. The company reflects the philosophy established by the founders, based on Psalm 68:11,
"The Lord gave the word and great was the company of those who published it."

Book design copyright © 2010 by Tate Publishing, LLC. All rights reserved.
Cover design by Kandi Evans
Interior design by Nathan Harmony

Published in the United States of America

ISBN: 978-1-61663-457-5
Religion: Christian Theology: General
10.05.13

Table of Contents

Foreword

Some books are important because they determine the spirit of an age. Other books are important because they define the spirit of an age. This book is important because it debunks the spirit of the age.

The title of this volume, *Christians in Hell*, is deliberately provocative (some might say outrageous). It needs to be so because it is one voice raised above the deafening din of many voices promoting false hopes of salvation. It is a voice raised against universalism, the unbiblical, soul-damning ethos of our age. That humanistic idea, made fashionable in the secular world of pop psychology in the 1967 book by Thomas Harris entitled *I'm OK—You're OK*, has crept—leaped is a better word—into Christendom. Monolithic forces in the church world are at work everywhere today promoting the idea that everyone is okay before God and that all are going to heaven without regard to what they believe and how they behave. God has given a clear message regarding the one and only way of salvation, as well as specific warnings against the purveyors of the false gospel that declares that anyone who says he believes in the Lord is saved.

We should not be surprised by such a state of affairs. When our Lord Himself announced that one of his twelve disciples would betray him, eleven pairs of eyes did not turn as one to stare at Judas. They did not recognize the apostasy in him. He looked like the eleven, talked like the eleven, acted like the eleven, and even held the responsible office of purse holder for the Lord and the twelve. He professed himself to be a believer and perhaps for some significant time until it was too late thought himself truly to be a follower of the Lord. But he was deceived and a deceiver. And so the Lord observed: "Ye are clean, but not all" (John 13:10). Sadly, many today are not "clean." They have put their trust in a false hope.

Though many profess to proclaim the truth and many more trust that they have a saving faith in the truth, the spirit of this age is one of confusion, deceit, and error. When a society becomes characterized by such rampant spiritual deceit threatening to sweep into hell untold millions who think they are headed to heaven, a Jeremiah must stand up and warn of impending tragedy. "Why will ye die?" the prophet asked the nation of Judah in the sixth century b.c. as the judgment of Babylonian captivity loomed. A much greater judgment—final and eternal—impends for many professing Christians today. Many who sincerely believe themselves to be real Christians are deceived regarding the substance of their faith and the destiny of their souls. This volume is the voice of a twenty-first-century Jeremiah crying out a loving plea to those lost and deceived souls to turn to the truth and shouting out a call to those who know the Lord to take up the warning as well. May this book be used of the Lord to stir up real believers to witness for the truth and to provoke professors to examine the validity of their faith.

—Philip K. Owen,
pastor and author of
the *Grace Notes* weekly devotional
(www.gbcurbana.com)

Introduction

I have been an ordained minister for more than thirty-five years. During that time, I have seen great changes take place in professing Christendom. In my youth, it seemed to me that most everyone who professed to be a Christian had a respect for the Bible as the unchanging Word of God. It seemed relatively easy to speak to just about anyone about Jesus Christ. Of course, not everyone would agree with what was said, but there seemed to be a general reverence for things "Christian" nevertheless.

Then came what now is known generically as the sixties, and things began to change very rapidly. Peace and love became the siren call. Self-expression became more important than "Thus saith the Lord." Men began to define Christianity culturally instead of biblically, even the professing church. In some circles, God was declared to be "dead," and Jesus was preached as someone less than divine. It was during this time that the movement to elevate man, the creature, to godhood gained momentum.

This downward spiral has continued and accelerated right into the twenty-first century. Today's Christianity is very different from the Christianity of my youth. While there has been a resurgence of evangelistic zeal in recent years, the substance and message of much of the current movement is not the same as the evangelism of the early twentieth century. The words used to describe the faith appear to be much the same on the surface, but the spirit behind the words is decidedly different. And the meanings of the words seem to be subject to private interpretation. As a consequence, rather than being defined by the eternal Word of God, what it means to be a Christian seems to be left to individual whim.

Because of this man-centered approach to defining Christianity, there is a much broader spectrum of society comfortable with claiming the name of Christ than in the past when becoming a Christian included the call to take up a personal cross daily and follow the example of Christ, including His separation from the world and suffering for the cause of God's truth. As a result, there is more religious activity taking place today than ever before. However, it appears to this Christian that much of this activity is man generated, not Spirit induced. Many are claiming that there is a "worldwide revival" taking place, that they have a plan to "win the world for Christ." However, in view of the Lord's teachings in Matthew 24-25, such claims lack credibility. The Lord said that when He returns, rather than a great revival, "the love of many shall wax cold" (Matthew 24:12). And He put this warning into practical perspective when He challenged His disciples (and us) with the sobering question "When the Son of man cometh, shall he find faith on the earth?" (Luke 18:8). The Apostle Paul, who was taught personally by the Lord

(Galatians 1:11- 12), confirmed this view when he told the Christians at Thessalonica that there would be a great "falling away" from God, i.e., gross apostasy, not a world-wide revival, right before the Lord returned to gather His Church to Himself for eternity (2 Thessalonians 2:3).

My personal perspective should be obvious by now. I believe we are in the last stages of the end times, which will culminate with the events detailed in the Revelation. If I and those of like persuasion are correct, then much of the religious activity we are witnessing is not true Spirit-generated revival but the "false incense" of the many false gospels being promoted today of which both the Lord and His apostles warned us. Consequently, in my opinion, what is being manifested in many of the disciples of these gospels is not the fruit of the Spirit, i.e., the fruit of true, saving faith, but the vain religious works of men and women who, while well intentioned and very religious, are, nevertheless, lost. In short, I believe we are in the day when men are saying, "peace and safety" when, in fact, the day of God's "sudden destruction" is right at hand, just as the Holy Spirit warned us through Paul's letter to the Thessalonians (1 Thessalonians 5:3).

Let me state plainly that this book is not about prophecy. I make no attempt to put forth any vain predictions as to the time or the events that may be taking place on earth when the Lord returns. All such efforts are to a lesser or greater degree folly, for only the Father knows His time (Mark 13:32). This book is intended to be neither a detailed exposition of the doctrines of the grace of God nor a comprehensive work on His great work of salvation. Rather, this book is intended to be a simple, heart-felt provocation to everyone who professes Jesus Christ as Lord to examine his faith in the light of "all the counsel of God" (Acts 20:27).

The writer of Hebrews exhorts us that it is the responsibility of every Christian to "consider one another to provoke unto love and to good works" (Hebrews 10:24). To that end, this book is intended to provoke all truly born-again Christians to be faithful, courageous witnesses to the world around them, zealous for the Lord and His glory, and faithful to their calling to be ambassadors for Christ.

However, the primary purpose of this work is to provoke to serious self-examination the multitudes of self-proclaimed "Christians" who may be merely professors of the Christian faith that sincerely believe they have been saved "from the wrath to come" (1 Thessalonians 1:10) but who are lost and headed for a hellish eternity. I do not intend to condemn anyone. I have no right to condemn. I am a sinner saved only by the grace of God myself. Rather, my sole desire is to stir up the minds and hearts of all who may read this book so that they might be certain that they have come to a true saving faith in Jesus Christ and will not be disappointed on Judgment Day.

I believe I have written this with the same sincere compassion and the same loving and concerned spirit with which the Apostle Paul provoked the people in the church at Corinth. And my exhortation is exactly the same:

> Examine yourselves, whether ye be in the faith; prove your own selves. Know ye not your own

selves, how that Jesus Christ is in you, except ye
be reprobates?

2 Corinthians 13:5

This work is about the most shocking truth the Lord
Jesus Christ ever taught. It is about the truth He revealed
in Matthew 7:21-23 and Luke 13:23-30 when He told
His disciples that on the Judgment Day, He will condemn to eternal damnation multitudes of shocked men
and women who sincerely thought themselves to be
Christians. But they were not, because they had trusted in
the false teachings of the religions of their day. They had
placed their trust in a false hope, their own good works,
rather than the sure hope of "the Lamb of God, which
taketh away the sins of the world" (John 1:29). It is a truth
that He emphasized throughout His ministry on earth.
It is a truth that continued to be emphasized throughout the ministries of His apostles. It is a truth that has
been passed on to all generations through the plain teachings of the Bible. Unfortunately, it is a truth that is being
neglected, even denied, by much of the professing church
of today. It is a truth we must understand, a warning that
should sober all of us.

May God use this work to both provoke and bless you.
May it be a helper to your faith as you prepare to meet
your God.

Christians in Hell?

Blasphemy? Heresy? No, as difficult as it may be to believe, this reality must be accepted and understood by every real Christian who would be an effective and faithful ambassador for his Lord, Jesus Christ. There will be "Christians" in hell!

God's Word assures the convicted sinner "That if thou shalt confess with thy mouth the Lord Jesus, and shalt believe in thine heart that God hath raised him from the dead, thou shalt be saved" (Romans 10:9). Yet, He warned His disciples (and us) that there is going to be a large group of people who will stand before Him on the Judgment Day who will have said these words and claimed Him as their Lord but will still be "dead in trespasses and sins" (Ephesians 2:1). Consequently, He will condemn them to eternal damnation. Listen to the Lord's own words as He describes this group in two different passages from the Gospel of Matthew, the gospel of the King of kings and Judge of all the earth.

> When the Son of man shall come in his glory, and all the holy angels with him, then shall he sit upon the

throne of his glory: And before him shall be gathered all nations: and he shall separate them one from another, as a shepherd divideth his sheep from the goats:

And he shall set the sheep on his right hand, but the goats on the left…Then shall he say also unto them on the left hand, Depart from me, ye cursed, into everlasting fire, prepared for the devil and his angels: For I was an hungered, and ye gave me no meat: I was thirsty, and ye gave me no drink: I was a stranger, and ye took me not in: naked, and ye clothed me not: sick, and in prison, and ye visited me not.

Then shall they also answer him, saying, Lord, when saw we thee and hungered, or athirst, or a stranger, or naked, or sick, or in prison, and did not minister unto thee?

Then shall he answer them, saying, verily I say unto you, Inasmuch as ye did it not to one of the least of these, ye did it not to me. And these shall go away into everlasting punishment: but the righteous into life eternal.

Matthew 25:31-33, 41-46

Not every one that saith unto me, Lord, Lord, shall enter into the kingdom of heaven; but he that doeth the will of my Father which is in heaven.

Many will say to me in that day, Lord, Lord, have we not prophesied in thy name? and in thy name have cast out devils? And in thy name done many wonderful works?

And then will I profess unto them, I never knew ye: depart from me, ye that work iniquity.

Matthew 7:21-23

Let's consider the scene the Lord describes in these two passages.

The day described by the Lord is the judgment that will take place at the end of the great Tribulation Period after the Lord returns in glory. It is described in detail in Revelation 19:11-20:6 and was foretold by the Lord in Matthew 24:27-31:

> For as the lightning cometh out of the east, and shineth even unto the west; so shall also the coming of the Son of man be ... Immediately after the tribulation of those days shall the sun be darkened, and the moon shall not give her light, and the stars shall fall from heaven, and the powers of the heavens shall be shaken: And then shall appear the sign of the Son of man in heaven: and then shall all the tribes of the earth mourn, and they shall see the Son of man coming in the clouds of heaven with power and great glory. And he shall send his angels with a great sound of a trumpet, and they shall gather together his elect from the four winds, from one end of heaven to the other.

Think of this. The world will have suffered through seven years of the worst tribulation ever known to man. Untold millions of people will have died as the result of war, famine, pestilences, violence, and religious persecution. At the midpoint of this divinely predestined and administered tribulation, two witnesses will be sent from heaven to preach the gospel of salvation by faith alone and warn men of the coming judgment of God. After three and one-half years of their faithful witnessing, the Beast, the head of the world's political system who will be indwelt by Satan, will be allowed by God to brutally slay them. Their dead bodies will be left to rot in the streets of Jerusalem to emphasize the fact that the Beast has no reverence for God, His messengers, or His people, and will violently put down any and all opposition to his evil reign. However, despite the Beast's bravado and carnal pride, after three days of the world's rejoicing over these deaths, God calls from heaven, "Come up hither." While all the world watches, these two messengers, who the Beast thought he had silenced forever, rise from their death; stand on their feet; and in their last and mightiest witness to the grace and power of God, ascend up to heaven in a cloud (Revelation 11:3-12).

Following this miraculous resurrection, God intensifies His judgment on sinful man for another three and one-half years. Then, finally, the event God's people had looked forward to for thousands of years will take place.

> And I saw heaven opened, and behold a white horse; and he that sat upon him was called Faithful and True, and in righteousness he doth judge and make war. His eyes were as a flame of fire, and on his head were many crowns; and he had a name written, that no man knew, but he himself. And he was clothed with a vesture dipped in blood: and his name is called The Word of God. And the armies which were in heaven followed him upon white horses, clothed in fine linen, white and clean. And out of his mouth goeth a sharp sword, that with it he should smite the nations: and he shall rule them

with a rod of iron: and he treadeth the winepress
of the fierceness and wrath of Almighty God. And
he hath on his vesture and on his thigh a name
written, King of kings, and Lord of lords.

Revelation 19:11-16

Given the awesome glory and power of God that had
been manifested by all of these things in the sight of all
men, you would expect absolute reverence to be manifested as men were gathered for the great judgment before
His throne (Romans 14:11). You might suppose that those
standing before the Lord would hold out some faint,
though vain, hope that a show of humility at this time
might possibly purchase for them some degree of mercy.

Yet, according to the Lord's own teachings, there will be
a group on that day of judgment who will be so hardened
in their sins, so deceived by their own self-righteousness,
that when their time to stand before the Lord comes they
will have the audacity to speak out against the Righteous
Judge, presumptuously challenging His verdicts and ques-
tioning His wisdom and justice (Matthew 7:13). At a time
when man's fear of and reverence for God should silence
all of his carnal, foolish, and worthless reasoning, these
religious unbelievers are so bold in their self-deceit that
they oppose the righteous judgment of Divinity!

Attempting to justify themselves they cry, "Lord, when
saw we thee an hungred, or athirst, or a stranger, or naked,
or sick, or in prison, and did not minister unto thee?"
(Matthew 25:44). The Lord's answer is simple and direct:

"Verily I say unto you, inasmuch as ye did *it* not to one of the least of these, ye did *it* not to me." (Matthew 25:45).

What a different spirit is this than that which characterizes those who truly know Jesus Christ as Lord and Savior. The true children of His kingdom are humbled in His presence, as was Ezekiel when called before His holy throne or John when the Lord appeared to him to give him His Revelation.

> As the appearance of the bow that is in the cloud in the day of rain, so *was* the appearance of the brightness round about. This *was* the appearance of the likeness of the glory of the LORD. And when I saw *it*, I fell upon my face.
>
> Ezekiel 1:28

> And when I saw him, I fell at his feet as dead.
>
> Revelation 1:17

In contrast, this group, when standing in the presence of the One who alone is to be exalted, exalt themselves! Rather than falling on their face in abject humility before holiness, these question the Lord's condemnation of their fruitlessness and pridefully recount their personal religious experiences and humanistic works. In one last vain attempt to avert His omniscient judgment of their manifold sins, they plead: "Lord, Lord, have we not prophesied in thy name? And in thy name have cast out devils? And in thy name done many wonderful works? (Matthew 7:22).

How they perfectly prove that "Before destruction the heart of man is haughty"(Proverbs 18:12a). Despite their protests and boastings, each one is held accountable for his own sins by the omnipotent Judge against whom they were committed. Each unbeliever stands spiritually naked before omniscience, stripped of all self-righteousness. The Judge examines everything in the light of His own infinite righteousness. Every sinful thought and intent of the heart is fully exposed and examined. Sin once thought to be hidden is now made public. Even "idle" thoughts that were considered to be of no consequence at the time they were formed are judged.[1]

In the end, no work of man satisfies Him. He declares all men's righteousness to be "filthy rags" (Isaiah 64:6) in comparison to His infinite holiness and just demands, and declares His final and perfect judgment: "There is none righteous, no, not one" (Romans 3:11).

Despite their desperate pleas and self-justification, the Lord's holy conclusion is blunt and final: "I never knew you: depart from me, ye that work iniquity." Their judgment is announced and executed immediately. "Depart from me, ye cursed, into everlasting fire, prepared for the devil and his angels" (Matthew 25:41). No excuses or rationalizations are accepted, no "scapegoats" allowed, no mercy shown. They are cast into the fires of eternal damnation as the Beast and False Prophet, the world's final religious leader, were before them (Revelations 20:12). The day they thought would be their coronation is the day of their eternal damnation. They are the self-deceived individuals to whom woe is ascribed in the prophecy of Amos 5:18-20:

Woe unto you that desire the day of the Lord! To what end *is* it for you? The day of the Lord *is* darkness, and not light. As if a man did flee from a lion, and a bear met him; or went into the house, and leaned his hand on the wall, and a serpent bit him. *Shall* not the day of the Lord *be* darkness, and not light? Even very dark, and no brightness in it?

A.B. Bruce, in his book *The Training of the Twelve*, comments on these in giving admonitions to those who are heavily involved in evangelistic works. He warns against several dangers, including pride from personal "success," the demeaning of others who are not so engaged or not as "successful." He ends his admonition as follows:

> Once more, they may fall into carnal security respecting their own spiritual state, deeming it impossible that any thing can go wrong with those who are so devoted, and whom God has so greatly owned. An obvious, as well as dangerous, mistake; for doubtless Judas took part in this Galilean mission, and, for aught we know to the contrary, was as successful as his fellow-disciples in casting out devils. Graceless men may for a season be employed as agents in promoting the work of grace in the hearts of others. Usefulness does not necessarily imply goodness, according to the teaching of Christ Himself. "Many," He declares in the Sermon on the Mount, "will say unto me on that day, Lord, Lord, did we not prophesy by Thy name, and by Thy name cast out devils, and by Thy name do many wonderful works?" And mark

the answer which He says He will give such. It is not: I call in question the correctness of your statement—that is tacitly admitted; it is, "I never knew you; depart from me, ye that work iniquity" (Matthew 7:23).[2]

Friends, the Lord Jesus Christ is God. He speaks only the truth. There is "no guile" in anything He says (1 Peter 2:22). That this solemn picture of the future is accurate is beyond doubt. This reality should greatly sober our thinking and influence our witnessing as we share with others the glorious salvation offered by God's grace through faith alone in Jesus Christ. And it should provoke all who claim the name of Christ to consider personally some very serious questions:

1. How could intelligent, well-meaning people be so utterly deceived?

Answer: Their faith was very real to them. They truly believed what they had been taught. Unfortunately, what they had been taught, believed, and ultimately trusted in for their salvation was wrong! They never realized that their faith was misplaced and unable to save them.

2. How could anyone live his life as a Christian without even an inkling of thought that his eternal destiny was not heaven but hell?

Answer: Because the heart of man is desperately wicked, especially deceitful to the one in whom it dwells (Jeremiah 17:9).

3. What influence could be so powerful and all-consuming as to make these religious-but-lost individuals continue their rebellion against the wisdom and dictates of our holy God even when standing before His very presence on that awesome day of judgment?

Answer: Man-centered religion. They had been ensnared by the smooth things that men had taught them, and had trusted in the man-centered and self-serving religion of their day. They had failed to reverence God's Holy Word, all of His Word rightly divided. They placed the authority of God's eternal truth below the thoughts of their own deceitful hearts, and their own personal and emotional religious experiences. In other words, they had trusted in their feelings and the teachings of their time that exalted man and man's reason over the eternal truth of God's Word. They had ignored, dismissed, demeaned, or neglected the holy and eternal truths of the sound doctrine of all the counsel of God. They had put their hope in self rather than the Lord Jesus Christ *alone*. In other words, without knowing it, they had denied the truth, the Word of God who alone can save.

You see, though the words of these people were Christian, they themselves were not. They were merely Christians in form only. Their lives witnessed the fact that they had never been saved, for the power and fruit of God's righteousness was not in them. By substituting their own works for Christ's, they had, in effect, rejected Him. Though He takes no pleasure in their damnation, He is bound by His own holiness to condemn all unbelief. "Shall not the Judge of all the earth do right?" (Genesis 18:25b).

4. Will I be among this group?

Answer: Only you with the Lord's help can determine this.

Hearing Only or Hearing and Doing?

The Difference between Eternal Death and Eternal Life

Matthew 7:21-23 clearly illustrates the irrefutable truth that justification is by faith alone. The works-based religions of man do not change his inherent sin nature nor purchase for him salvation. They only embolden his self-confidence and his rebellion against the Lord and His truth.

While it is sad to view this group of deceived individuals being cast into hell by the Lord, you must remember that God is a righteous judge who judges with all wisdom to satisfy His perfect justice. In other words, He does not make any mistakes. "Shall not the Judge of all the earth do right?"(Genesis 18:25b). "But we are sure that the judgment of God is according to truth" (Romans 2:2a).

Their own behavior justifies His wisdom in damning them. Their actions before His throne are the undeniable evidence of their true nature, the proof His judgment is right. They manifest the unchanging character of religious unbelievers of all ages that Paul detailed in his exhortations to those who were dwelling among the Christians in Rome.

> But after thy hardness and impenitent heart trea-surest up unto thyself wrath against the day of wrath and revelation of the righteous judgment of God; Who will render to every man according to his deeds: To them who by patient continuance in well doing seek for glory and honour and immor-tality, eternal life: But unto them that are conten-tious, and do not obey the truth, but obey unrigh-teousness, indignation and wrath, Tribulation and anguish, upon every soul of man that doeth evil, of the Jew first, and also of the Gentile... For there is no respect of persons with God... For not the hearers of the law *are* just before God, but the do-ers of the law shall be justified.
>
> Romans 2:5-13

These poor lost souls are so blind to their sins and their disregard for the truth that they callously reject the Lord's wisdom even on the Judgment Day! They were deceived into believing their religious experiences were evidence of true salvation, but, in fact, they were never saved. They substituted their own righteousness for God's and nur-tured and served their own sense of truth rather than sub-mitting to Him who alone is truth and to His Word, the Bible. They accepted bits and pieces of His Word as it was convenient for them, but they refused to submit to "all the counsel of God" (Acts 20:27). Consequently, they never fully comprehended their sinful nature, never sincerely repented of their sins, and never came to know the Lord Jesus Christ as their Savior nor truly submitted to Him as the Master of their life. Thinking themselves "to be wise, they became fools," (Romans 1:22) always, though not always consciously, arguing with God, attempting to redefine and twist His Word and ways into doctrines acceptable to their fallible, finite minds!

A scriptural rule of thumb for saving faith:

Referencing Romans 3:18-19:

> There is no fear of God before their eyes. Now we know that what things soever the law saith, it saith to them who are under the law: that every mouth may be stopped, and all the world may become guilty before God.

D. Martyn Lloyd-Jones gave a very simple rule of thumb for evaluating when a person becomes a true believer. Though simple, it rings true to the spiritual, discerning ear, especially in view of the undeniable character of this group before us:

> But Paul now points out to them that when you realize what the Law is truly saying to you, the result is that "every mouth shall be stopped." You are rendered speechless. You are not a Christian unless you have been made speechless! How do you know whether you are a Christian or not? It is that you "stop talking." The trouble with the non-Christian is that he goes on talking. He says "I do not see

this, I do not see that. After all I am doing this and I am doing that." He is still talking.

How do you know whether a man is a Christian? The answer is that his mouth is "shut." I like this forthrightness of the Gospel. People need to have their mouths shut, "stopped." They are for ever talking about God, and criticizing God, and pontificating about what God should or should not do, and asking "Why does God allow this and that?" You do not begin to be a Christian until your mouth is shut, is stopped, and you are speechless and have nothing to say. You put forth all of your arguments, and produce all your righteousness; then the Law speaks and it all withers to nothing—becomes "filthy rags" and "dung," and you have nothing to say. [1]

There is a huge difference between the true believer, and the mere professor of the Christian faith. The true believer is both a hearer and a doer of God's Word,[2] the mere professor is a hearer only, especially when God's Word provokes, rebukes, or condemns him. This difference distinguishes lip service from heart service, and superficial humanistic religious faith that ultimately leads to eternal damnation, from true saving faith that honors God, transforms the believer into a new creature, and secures for him eternal life.

To be a hearer of religious talk is not only easy today, it is popular. Surveys tell us that the number of people who believe they are going to go to heaven when they die is rapidly increasing. In one of its evening TV broadcasts in the summer of 2006, NBC news announced the results of a recently released Baylor University survey. Though the survey was very extensive in dealing with Americans' attitudes and beliefs concerning many aspects of religion and faith, the anchorman focused on three significant statistics:

- 92% of Americans believe in God (or some higher Power)
- 75% of Americans believe their family will be in heaven
- 64% of Americans believe their friends will be in heaven

However, despite this brash public confidence, the actual number who are really going to heaven and that actually submit to God's truth and come to Him His way are only a small portion of these. In fact, as previously mentioned, when reflecting on the apostasy, or the great falling away from God and His truth that characterizes this present time (2 Thessalonians 2:3), Jesus asked His disciples, "when the Son of man cometh, shall he find faith on the earth" (Luke 18:8b).

A 2006 survey conducted by the Barna Group, a California-based Christian research firm, underscores Christ's remark and provides further perspective on today's "believers." When Barna surveyed Americans on their view of Satan, the following was revealed.[3]

- 55% view Satan as symbolic of evil rather than a real entity

- 45% of born-again Christians don't believe Satan is real

- 68% of Catholics think of Satan only as a symbol

Can anyone be truly saved who does not believe in a literal Satan? If someone believes that Satan is not real, then he must also believe that Jesus was a liar, because Jesus taught about a literal Satan more than any other person in the Bible. If Jesus was a liar, then He died for His own sins, not for ours. And if Jesus did not die for our sins, then we are all still guilty before God and doomed to an eternal hell.

Let us not be deceived. Could a symbolic Satan be chained for a thousand years, then released to administer one last temptation to sinful man before the Great Judgment (Revelation 20:2)? Could a symbolic Satan be cast into the lake of fire (Revelation 20:10)? Could the Christ, who is God, lie?

Yes, adopting the title of "Christian" is very easy today. It is easy to enjoy the charismatic preaching of easy-believism, to participate in the social activities of an active and growing church organization, and to take advantage of the privileges of church membership. It is easy to join the crowd and claim the name of Christ.

But simply proclaiming the name of Christ is not evidence of salvation. Salvation is not the adoption of the title Christian. Salvation is a new life, a transformed life, and a new way of living. That's the difference between a purely religious self-serving faith and true God-honoring saving faith. For though it is easy to become "Christianized," adopting one of the many popular man-centered gospels being preached today, it is not easy to sacrifice yourself willingly and wholly for the cause of Christ and the true gospel. Yet this is exactly what the Lord requires of all His true children:

> And when he had called the people *unto him* with his disciples also, he said unto them, Whosoever will come after me, let him deny himself, and take up his cross, and follow me. For whosoever will save his life shall lose it; but whosoever shall lose his life for my sake and the gospel's, the same shall save it. For what shall it profit a man, if he shall gain the whole world, and lose his own soul? Or what shall a man give in exchange for his soul? Whosoever therefore shall be ashamed of me and of my words in this adulterous and sinful generation; of him also shall the Son of man be ashamed, when he cometh in the glory of his Father with the holy angels.
>
> Mark 8:34-38

A.W. Tozer, early twentieth century evangelist and Bible scholar, once said, "One hundred religious persons knit into a unity by careful organizations do not constitute a church any more than eleven dead men make a football team. The first requisite is life, always."[4] And while that life is indeed a life of joy unspeakable and divine peace that is beyond human understanding, it is also a life of self-sacrifice.

The Power and Deceit of Man-Centered Religion

The blinding power of man-centered religion, which feeds the desires of the carnal, unregenerate heart, combined with the deadly snare of self-deceit, which humanistic works produce, creates the large and growing group that I call the religious lost. Man has learned to please himself and his peers even as he willingly, though for the most part ignorantly, rejects the demands of the God he claims to love and serve.

> Wherefore the Lord said, Forasmuch as this people draw near *me* with their mouth, and with their lips do honour me, but have removed their heart far from me, and their fear toward me is taught by the precept of men: Therefore, behold, I will proceed to do a marvellous work among this people, *even* a marvellous work and a wonder: for the wisdom of their wise *men* shall perish, and the understanding of their prudent *men* shall be hid.
>
> Isaiah 29:13-14

And he said unto them, Ye are they which justify yourselves before men; but God knoweth your hearts: for that which is highly esteemed among men is abomination in the sight of God.

Luke 16:15

The Confusion in Today's Professing Church

The great confusion that will occur at the Great Judgment is rooted in the great confusion that exists in professing Christendom today. In his effort to create a superficial ecumenical unity among the many different and conflicting beliefs that exist in what is called the church today, religious man has set aside the glory of God and the truth of God's Holy Word in favor of evangelical expediency. This has resulted in many different gospels being preached that are not the true gospel at all. As a result, there are multitudes of professing "Christians" who have sincerely placed their faith in the Christ their leaders have exalted who is not the Christ of the Bible, the Christ who saves!

This is exactly what the Lord was warning His disciples about in Matthew 7. If you will look at the full context of His warning, you will see that the real problem the Lord was addressing was the false teachers and their erroneous doctrines that would lead these religious-but-lost individuals away from the truth. This focus continued to the end of His ministry on earth.

And as he sat upon the mount of Olives, the disciples came unto him privately, saying, Tell us, when shall these things be? And what *shall be* the sign of thy coming, and of the end of the world? And Jesus answered and said unto them, Take heed that no man deceive you. For many shall come in my name, saying, I am Christ; and shall deceive many.

Matthew 24:3-5

One day the vanity of the proponents of the man-centered religions that are drawing untold multitudes to hell will be fully exposed. At the Great Judgment the deceits of these false gospels will be revealed and the vain hope of their disciples destroyed. They will be exposed as merely religious unbelievers and, in some cases, charlatans who knowingly made "merchandise" of God's people to satisfy their own sinful covetousness and fulfill their own greedy lusts.[1]

For nothing is secret, that shall not be made manifest; neither *any thing* hid, that shall not be known and come abroad. Take heed therefore how ye hear: for whosoever hath, to him shall be given; and whosoever hath not, *from him shall be taken even that which he seemeth to have.*

Luke 8:17-18 (italics added)

The doctrines that deceive the religious lost are those that offer a wide gate and a broad way to enter into salvation and live as a Christian. This is a direct contradiction of the true way of salvation; it is a way that leads to destruction. In other words, it is a counterfeit, that is to say, a false gospel.

Enter ye in at the strait gate: for wide *is* the gate, and broad *is* the way, that leadeth to destruction,

Daniel P. Franklin

and many there be which go in thereat: Because strait *is* the gate, and narrow *is* the way, which leadeth unto life, and few there be that find it. Beware of false prophets, which come to you in sheep's clothing, but inwardly they are ravening wolves. Ye shall know them by their fruits…Every tree that bringeth not forth good fruit is hewn down, and cast into the fire. Wherefore by their fruits ye shall know them.

Matthew 7:13-20

This teaching has become the reality of the church since Christ's ascension into heaven. Attempts to deceive men into following error rather than the truth began immediately and continue to this day. In obedience to the Lord, Peter not only warned the early church about the many false teachers of his day but also about the danger of being self-deceived by perverting God's Word to suit themselves when they found its truths difficult to understand or accept:

But there were false prophets also among the people, even as there shall be false teachers among you, who privily shall bring in damnable heresies, even denying the Lord that bought them, and bring upon themselves swift destruction. And many shall follow their pernicious ways; by reason of whom the way of truth shall be evil spoken of. And through covetousness shall they with feigned words make merchandise of you: whose judgment now of a long time lingereth not, and their damnation slumbereth not.

2 Peter 2:1-3

Nevertheless we, according to his promise, look for new heavens and a new earth, wherein dwelleth righteousness. Wherefore, beloved, seeing that ye look for such things, be diligent that ye may be found of him in peace, without spot, and blameless. And account *that* the longsuffering of our Lord *is* salvation; even as our beloved brother Paul also according to the wisdom given unto him hath written unto you; As also in all *his* epistles, speaking in them of these things; in which are some things hard to be understood, which they that are unlearned and unstable wrest (to twist or distort), as *they do* also the other scriptures, unto their own destruction.

2 Peter 3:13-16

Jude also witnessed the fulfillment of the Lord's prophecy regarding the proliferation and effect of false teachers and their teachings. Virtually his entire letter was an exhortation to his brethren to "earnestly contend for the faith which was once delivered to the saints" against those who would come into their fellowships and undermine real saving faith by "turning the grace of our God into lasciviousness (wanton lustfulness, sinfulness), and denying [i.e. rebelling against the rule of] the only Lord God, and our Lord Jesus Christ" (Jude 1:3-4).

Paul too in exhorting Timothy to faithfully carry on the preaching and defense of the gospel instructed him to "Hold fast the form of sound words, which thou hast heard of me, in faith and love which is in Christ Jesus. That good thing which was committed unto thee keep by the Holy Ghost which dwelleth in us" (2 Timothy 1:13-14).

Why was Paul so specific and dogmatic in instructing Timothy to maintain even "the form of sound words?" Because words can convey either truth or error, depending on how they are used and understood. In other words, how the gospel of the saving grace of God in Jesus Christ is presented is important. Every doctrine must be clearly stated, then guarded with all spiritual diligence and zeal. Yet today many churches believe such faithfulness to the declared Word of God is not only unnecessary but, in some strange sense, may not be truly "Christian!"

A Sobering Example of Man-Centered Religion

The Foundation Magazine is a periodical that brings the events and personalities that are influencing professing Christendom today under the light of the eternal Word of God. For many months, this publication outlined the differing beliefs of many religious denominations. The July-August 2006 issue presented an outline of the beliefs of the United Church of Christ. The following quotation[2] illustrates the apparent disregard many organizations that are perceived by most to be very "traditional" in their beliefs have for the Bible, its plain teachings, and "the faith which was once delivered unto the saints" (Jude 1:3), the narrow way which leadeth unto life.

> Every member is free to follow his own set of beliefs:
> "As individual members, we are free to believe and act in accordance with our perception of God's will for our lives...There is no

centralized authority or hierarchy that can impose any doctrine or form of worship on its
members." (United Church of Christ Web site,
October 1998: www.ucc.org)

This statement of faith does not read like a typi-
cal doctrinal statement and cannot be understood
by a literal interpretation of its words. The United
Church of Christ believes that every generation of
the church should "rethink and then rephrase its
faith." Furthermore, it insists that what the church
fathers taught is irrelevant today. What they believed was fine for them, but what Christians believe today must be decided for themselves. Thus,
they seek "an affirmation of our own which sets
forth what being Christian means to us and not
to some long-past time." The current statement of
faith for the United Church of Christ is merely this
generation's way of expressing itself: "Some day it
too will be out of date, but right now it is the latest,
freshest affirmation of our common belief." (*United
Church of Christ, History and Program*, pages 37-39)

To the undiscerning ear, this may sound very reasonable,
even spiritual. After all, the language and culture of every
generation is, indeed, somewhat different. Surely a new
affirmation statement is needed to make the fundamentals of the faith understandable. However, it is not an
affirmation of "the faith which was once delivered unto
the saints," i.e. the saving faith of the Bible, that is being
affirmed by the members of this organization. Rather, it
is the affirmation of their own personal understanding

of faith that is being affirmed. It seems that the United Church of Christ encourages this because it does not believe that the Bible is truly the Word of God! I quote again from the Foundation article.

> The United Church of Christ does not believe in the verbal plenary inspiration of Scripture. To them, the Bible is only one of many ways in which God has expressed Himself throughout history. God's expression of Himself to man is merely "epitomized in the Scriptures." Thus, when the United Church refers to God's Word being spoken in the Scriptures, it means God has spoken through the vehicle of the Bible but not in the plain sense of the language of the Bible. To know what God has actually said, His Word must be mined out of the Bible through the techniques of literary criticism. The Bible must be examined by experts in history, language, archaeology and the sacred books of other religions in order to weed out all the things that are not the Word of God and to understand what God's current message is to the church:
> "The United Church of Christ does not regard the writers of the Bible as having been protected supernaturally from reporting events erroneously or setting forth inadequate and untrue philosophies. It is said in the Book of Joshua (10:12-13), for instance, that: Joshua ... said in the sight of Israel, Sun, stand thou still ... and the sun stood still ... and did not hasten to go down for about a whole day. There has been no day like it before or since. This is plainly folklore, most interesting

to any hearer, but imaginative beyond the limits which a modern historian would impose on himself." (*The United Church of Christ*, page 49)

"Take the Christmas story in Luke, for example…there are few adult members of the United Church of Christ who believe that angels, such as the medieval artists were fond of depicting, actually appeared from heaven and talked in Aramaic with a group of shepherds about the birth in the stable. What then is to be done with the story? Some denominations take the attitude that the fathers knew better than we, and that the story should be accepted as part of the belief of the church although we cannot believe it as individual Christians. This seems like an invitation to schizophrenia…The United Church of Christ holds affectionately to the Lucan account…but in any moment of reflection carefully distinguishes between the true kernel of the story and the elaborations of devoted fancy." (*The United Church of Christ*, page 80)

To the United Church of Christ, the Bible only contains the Word of God in a vague way. It teaches that God uses the Bible to communicate His Word in a fresh way to each new generation. Thus, the words contained in the Bible are not important. It only matters how God uses those words to enlighten those who happen to be reading them. "There is yet more light and truth to break forth from God's holy word…The study of the scriptures is not limited by past interpretations, but it is pursued with expectancy for new insight and help for living today." (UCC Web site)

The Holy Spirit, then, becomes important to the discovery of what God is saying through the Bible. The Holy Spirit does not appear to be a distinct person. He is instead referred to as "the name we give to God when he comes to us in this way" (page 50). What way is that? That is any experience in life which one feels has been caused by the direct hand of God. Such experiences result in "the glow of the soul," a phrase not taken from Scripture but from a playwright, yet equated with a Latin phrase out of church history; the *testimonium Sancti Spiritus internum* or the "testimony (witness) of the Holy Spirit within."

So how can a man know what God is saying through the Bible? As he critically analyzes the Bible, God (i.e. the Holy Spirit) will touch a man's mind, and the resulting illumination, or glow of his soul, will indicate to the man what God is saying. This is a very free and subjective method of discovering God's Word contained within the Bible. It obviously leaves revelation open-ended and results in a wide variety of interpretations.

By including the above representations regarding the doctrinal beliefs of the national United Church of Christ organization, I am not saying that all who worship within this denomination are unbelievers. Nor am I saying that all United Church of Christ members or congregations strictly adhere to or even agree with the above stated beliefs. However, I will say that those who do espouse the above doctrines and beliefs hold a view of God and the Bible that undermines true faith and erodes real confidence in

God and the salvation He has provided in His Son, Jesus Christ. Such a view subjects the Holy Scriptures to man's finite understanding and contradicts the view held by the apostles who walked with and were taught personally by Jesus Christ during His time on earth:

> We have also a more sure word of prophecy; where-unto ye do well that ye take heed, as unto a light that shineth in a dark place, until the day dawn, and the day star arise in your hearts: Knowing this first, that no prophecy of the scripture is of any private interpretation. For the prophecy came not in old time by the will of man: but holy men of God spake *as they were* moved by the Holy Ghost.
>
> 2 Peter 1:19-21

Turning from the Word of God and trusting in carnal self-enlightenment, i.e. private interpretation, is not a new phenomenon. It is, in my opinion, the "broad way that leadeth to destruction" traveled by those in every generation who turn from God's truth to trust in their own carnal wisdom, thereby denying the truth and walking in their own way according to their own will. What an offense to God, who makes it plain that obedience to His Word is more important than just "claiming" His name through claiming to be a Christian. "I will worship toward thy holy temple, and praise thy name for thy lovingkindness and for thy truth: for thou hast magnified thy word above all thy name" (Psalm 138:2).

God's commands are not optional. They are to be obeyed. God's truth is not an alternative way of thinking or perceiving things. It is absolute, the only standard against which all men will be measured. Yet, as the above implies, many who profess to be Christians do not hold this view. The following quotation from the introductory remarks from an Easter sermon by John Piper[3] illustrates the unholy attitude this error can engender in those who hold to it.

> Today the assumption is not that there are natural laws outside of me forbidding the resurrection of Jesus, but there is a personal law inside of me that says: I don't have to adapt my life to anything I don't find helpful. Or you could state it another way: Truth for me is what I find acceptable and helpful.
>
> Now with that assumption in place, and that inner law in place, it doesn't matter whether Jesus rose from the dead, because, whether he did or didn't, my issue is: Do I care? Do I find that idea helpful? Do I feel that it helps me flourish as a human being? And if it seems like it doesn't, then I will just view it the way I view UFOs and possible life in some distant galaxy—I just don't need to bother with it. If it helps you, that's fine; but don't press it on me.

While Piper was speaking to the specific doctrine of the literal resurrection of Jesus Christ, which is the linchpin of the Christian faith, the attitude he condemned in his comments is the inevitable fruit of the erroneous doctrine of man-centered religion that instructs fallible man to bring his own private interpretation to the infallible Word of God, i.e. to accept or reject what he feels is useful or not useful to his own self-determined purposes and lifestyle. When this happens, God is no longer the sovereign King of kings. Rather, the benevolent, holy Creator is rejected as Lord and Master and treated as the servant of the unthankful and sinfully presumptuous creature.

I once read a statement C. H. Spurgeon made in defense of the eternal Word of God as he challenged those who would "pick and choose" what parts of the Word were applicable to them and what parts, in their opinion, were not relevant to their times: "What! Think ye the Word of God to be a nose of clay that can be shaped to fit the face of each new generation?" The Lord, the Great Judge, has warned us against such insubordinate self-determination throughout His holy Word: "Ye shall not do after all *the things* that we do here this day, every man whatsoever *is* right in his own eyes" (Deuteronomy 12:8).

> Think not that I am come to destroy the law, or the prophets: I am not come to destroy, but to fulfil. For verily I say unto you, Till heaven and earth pass, one jot or one tittle shall in no wise pass from the law, till all be fulfilled. Whosoever therefore shall break one of these least commandments, and shall teach men so, he shall be called the least in the kingdom of heaven: but whosoever shall do and teach *them*, the same shall be called great in the kingdom of heaven. For I say unto you, That except your righteousness shall exceed *the righteousness* of the scribes and Pharisees, ye shall in no case enter into the kingdom of heaven.
>
> Matthew 5:17-20

He that rejecteth me, and receiveth not my words, hath one that judgeth him: the word that I have spoken, the same shall judge him in the last day.

John 12:48

For I testify unto every man that heareth the words of the prophecy of this book, If any man shall add unto these things, God shall add unto him the plagues that are written in this book: And if any man shall take away from the words of the book of this prophecy, God shall take away his part out of the book of life, and out of the holy city, and *from* the things which are written in this book.

Revelation 22:18-19

There is not a simpler, nor a more profound insight into the self-deceit that is consuming modern religious man than this: "He that trusteth in his own heart is a fool" (Proverbs 28:26a). Looking to his own wisdom to comprehend God and order his life, unregenerate man has become a fool. Not having the Spirit to guide him, he labors under the false notion that he can understand the infinite God and His ways with his own finite mind. Trusting in his own temporal wisdom, he thinks he can discover God's eternal truth. He can't.

But the natural man receiveth not the things of the Spirit of God: for they are foolishness unto him: neither can he know *them*, because they are spiritually discerned.

1 Corinthians 2:14

Can Words Alone Save?

God communicates by words. It is not insignificant that the Savior is named the "Word of God," the One who communicates to us the nature and eternal purposes of God. "In the beginning was the Word, and the Word was with God, and the Word was God... And the Word was made flesh, and dwelt among us, (and we beheld his glory, the glory as of the only begotten of the Father) full of grace and truth" (John 1:1, 14).

> God, who at sundry times and in divers manners spake in time past unto the fathers by the prophets, Hath in these last days spoken unto us by *his* Son, whom he hath appointed heir of all things, by whom also he made the worlds; Who being the brightness of *his* glory, and the express image of his person, and upholding all things by the word of his power, when he had by himself purged our sins, sat down on the right hand of the Majesty on high; Being made so much better than the angels, as he hath by inheritance obtained a more excellent name than they.
>
> Hebrews 1:1-4

Human beings also communicate by words. It should go without saying that the words used to preach and teach salvation are immeasurably important. How the words used by a preacher in his presentation of the gospel are defined dictates how the listening sinner (or believer) views God and what he believes about sin and salvation. A wrong presentation or emphasis will result in the hearer having a wrong understanding of the words of faith. This will inevitably lead to a wrong understanding of faith itself and to a false hope.

To be specific, if a real Christian were asked for his definition of grace, most likely he would give a definition that directly or indirectly suggests "unmerited favor." To the true believer, grace is the inestimable love and favor God bestows on him according to His own purposes, without regard to anything the believer was, is, or will ever be and without respect to anything he has done, is doing, or ever will do. Grace is unfathomable but very real. It is the basis for the Christian's peace and joy.

But what if a mere professor of the faith, i.e. someone who claims the name of Christ but whose faith rests on some mixture of faith plus human works rather than the finished and complete cross work of Christ, were asked to define grace? He might offer something like Merriam-Webster dictionary's definition: "unmerited *help* given to people by God (as in overcoming temptation)" [italics added]. Or, he might offer a definition relating to man's religious traditions such as "the ability received through church rites and sacraments to produce good *works* that please God." While these may seem to be minor differences to some, they most certainly are not.

One's concept of God determines his concept of God's grace which dictates the nature of his faith. Saving faith is trusting wholly and only in God's gracious provisions. It honors Him and appropriates His eternal peace.[1] In other words, it saves.

> But God, who is rich in mercy, for his great love wherewith he loved us, Even when we were dead in sins, hath quickened us together with Christ, (by grace ye are saved;) And hath raised *us* up together, and made *us* sit together in heavenly *places* in Christ Jesus: That in the ages to come he might shew the exceeding riches of his grace in *his* kindness toward us through Christ Jesus. For by grace are ye saved through faith; and that not of yourselves: *it is* the gift of God: Not of works, lest any man should boast.
>
> Ephesians 2:4-9

A faith that in principle or practice rests to any degree on personal good works not only dishonors God but demeans the finished cross work of Christ. It leaves its disciple in his sins, hopelessly lost. Put simply, the difference between a faith founded on grace alone and one based to any degree on man's works is the difference between salvation and damnation, sure hope and vain hope, heaven and hell.

In his work, *All the Last Words of Saints and Sinners*, Herbert Lockyer gathered together hundreds of testimonies that shed light on the true nature of the dying faith of its subjects. The following quotes taken from this work clearly illustrate that a faith that rests on man's good works or on the sacraments of religious institutions is a vain and empty hope.

> History speaks of Louis XV as the most sensual and depraved of all French monarchs. Vice, in manifold forms, had entered into the depravity of his unlicensed pleasure, yet as this one died, he tried to varnish his sinful life:
> I have been a great sinner, doubtless, but I have ever observed Lent with a most scrupulous exactness. I have caused more than a hundred thousand masses to be said for the repose of unhappy souls, so that I flatter myself I have not been a very bad Christian.

Isn't it amazing that religious works can give a poor, lost sinner false confidence? Contrast the deceived sinner's foolish testimony given above with that of the following testimonies of two real Christians quoted in the same work.

> T.E. Bond was not only a physician but a minister and editor. He died in 1856, leaving the world this farewell message:
> What is victory over death? Is it not the victory over the dread of death? Is it not the victory of patience under the sufferings which precede death? Is it not the victory of resignation in the prospect of death? Is it not the victory of faith, which looks beyond death, and trusts all to Christ?
> Francia Gamba, the martyr burned at the stake in 1554, was presented with a wooden cross by a monk, but rejected it saying: "My mind is so full of

the real merits of Christ as I die that I want not a piece of senseless stick to put me in mind of Him."[2]

How foolish are man's ways when placed before God's truth. How can men trust in symbols, relics, idols, or any work of their own hands when God condemns such things throughout His holy Word?

> Thou shalt not make unto thee any graven image, or any likeness *of any thing* that *is* in heaven above, or that *is* in the earth beneath, or that *is* in the water under the earth: Thou shalt not bow down thyself to them, nor serve them: for I the LORD thy God *am* a jealous God, visiting the iniquity of the fathers upon the children unto the third and fourth *generation* of them that hate me;
>
> Exodus 20:4-5

> Every man is brutish by *his* knowledge; every founder is confounded by the graven image: for his molten image *is* falsehood, and *there is* no breath in them. They *are* vanity, the work of errors: in the time of their visitation they shall perish.
>
> Jeremiah 51:18

> And the rest of the men which were not killed by these plagues yet repented not of the works of their hands, that they should not worship devils, and idols of gold, and silver, and brass, and stone, and of wood: which neither can see, nor hear, nor walk: Neither repented they of their murders, nor of their sorceries, nor of their fornication, nor of their thefts.
>
> Revelation 9:20-21

This chapter might have begun: "If you ask a truly *born-again* Christian …" But the term "born-again" has been applied to so many different things in today's religious world that its true meaning has been virtually lost in many circles.

To be born again as the Lord used the term in John 3:3 means to be regenerated, to be "born anew" into the family of God. It means to be spiritually crucified and raised from death to new life in Christ by faith in His cross work alone, to be fully washed from all sin, to be justified, that is, to be declared righteous before a holy and just God, and to be sanctified wholly by the work of God's own Holy Spirit according to His eternal purposes and sovereign will.[3] The Bible teaches that all of this is required to be saved from eternal damnation.

To be truly saved is to receive the very life of Christ. To be truly saved is to be changed from a self-centered and damned sinner into an eternally secure child of God and joint heir with Christ of all spiritual blessings.[4] To be truly born again is to become "a new creature: old things are passed away; behold, all things are become new" (2 Corinthians 5:17). In other words, to be born again is to be raised from spiritual death to spiritual life. The result is a transformed life, a new life which results in God-glorifying changes in personal values, desires, friendships, and behavior, i.e. lifestyle.

The view of man-centered religion regarding what it means to be "born again," however, contrasts sharply with this Scripture-based view. In much of today's professing church, the term "born again" is used to describe acts of mere self-reformation, psychological rationalization of personal sin, individual enlightenment, or emotional responses to emotional appeals. In other parts of the religious world, it is used to describe participation in various rites and sacrament-based religious ceremonies.

Given the confusion on these (and many other) basic truths of salvation, it is no wonder so many conflicts with the declared Word of God in both doctrine and practice exist within today's professing church. And these differences are of eternal importance. They color all aspects of saving faith from the most basic doctrines of how men are saved to the modes and means of worship and evangelism, to the Christian's temporal responsibilities and relationship with the world in which he lives.

This confusion has developed because of today's unholy movement to minimize doctrinal teaching in favor of what in many cases must be described as merely emotion-provoking Christianized entertainment. As a result of this trend, many beliefs that were once widely understood and reverently defended by Bible-believing Christians have fallen by the wayside, set aside by the evangelists of today's man-centered gospels. As a result of this failure to teach, defend, and submit to the Word's clear and eternal sound doctrine,[5] much of the modern, professing church has created its own "form of godliness" (2 Timothy 3:5) to support its own self-determined purposes. Utilizing secular marketing techniques, it has promoted this form and generated impressive growth in religious professions of salvation and church memberships. Unfortunately, the evidence of true salvation and sincere discipleship is conspicuously absent from large numbers of these supposedly enlightened converts. A.W. Tozer warned the church about this dangerous movement away from the preaching and teaching of sound doctrine over fifty years ago. His words still ring true today.

> It is now common practice in most evangelical churches to offer the people, especially the young people, a maximum of entertainment and a minimum of serious instruction. It is scarcely possible in most places to get anyone to attend a meeting where the only attraction is God. One can only conclude that God's professed children are bored with Him, for they must be wooed to the meeting with a stick of striped candy in the form of religious movies, games and refreshments...
>
> Any objection to the carryings on of our present golden-calf Christianity is met with the triumphant reply, "But we are winning them!" And winning them to what? To true discipleship? To cross-carrying? To self-denial? To separation from the world? To crucifixion of the flesh? To holy living? To nobility of character? To a despising of the world's treasures? To hard self-discipline? To love for God? To total committal to Christ? Of course the answer to all these questions is *no*.[6]

A commentary was published on the Internet[7] that outlined some of the findings of a multiyear study on the effectiveness of the programs and philosophy of ministry of one of the flagships of the Church Growth Movement.

The following excerpt from this commentary provides valuable perspective for the concerns expressed above.

> For most of a generation evangelicals have been romanced by the "seeker sensitive" movement spawned by Willow Creek Community Church in Chicago. The guru of this movement is Bill Hybels. He and others have been telling us for decades to throw out everything we have previously thought and been taught about church growth and replace it with a new paradigm, a new way to do ministry.
>
> Perhaps inadvertently, with this "new wave" of ministry came a de-emphasis on taking personal responsibility for Bible study combined with an emphasis on felt-needs based "programs" and slick marketing.
>
> The size of the crowd rather than the depth of the heart determined success...We were told that preaching was out, relevance was in. Doctrine didn't matter nearly as much as innovation...The mention of sin, salvation and sanctification were taboo and replaced by Starbucks, strategy and sensitivity.
>
> Thousands of pastors hung on every word that emanated from the lips of the church growth experts...The promise was clear: thousands of people and millions of dollars couldn't be wrong. Forget what people need, give them what they want...If you dared to challenge the "experts" you were immediately labeled as a "traditionalist," a throwback to the 50s, a stubborn dinosaur unwilling to change with the times.
>
> All that changed recently.
>
> Willow Creek has released the results of a multi-

year study on the effectiveness of their programs and philosophy of ministry. The study's findings are in a new book titled *Reveal: Where Are You?*,[8] co-authored by Cally Parkinson and Greg Hawkins, executive pastor of Willow Creek Community Church…it seems that the "experts" were wrong.

The report reveals that most of what they have been doing for these many years and what they have taught millions of others to do is not producing solid disciples of Jesus Christ. Numbers yes, but not disciples. It gets worse. Hybels laments:

"Some of the stuff that we have put millions of dollars into thinking it would really help our people grow and develop spiritually, when the data actually came back it wasn't helping people that much. Other things that we didn't put that much money into and didn't put much staff against is stuff our people are crying out for."

If you simply want a crowd, the "seeker sensitive" model produces results. If you want solid, sincere, mature followers of Christ, it's a bust.

Mere words, formulas, programs, etcetera, are not a substitute for the preaching and sound teaching of the Word of God. Man-centered religion is very good at creating forms of godliness, i.e. "smooth things" (Isaiah 30:10) with which both regenerate and unregenerate men are comfortable. However, these forms are void of the power to save and, thereby, transform lives. God saves through the preaching of His Word,[9] "the faith once delivered to the saints" (Jude 1:3). This will never change. Nor will the truth in Paul's exhortation to Timothy ever change. It is as applicable to ministers today as it was when it was first written:

> I charge *thee* therefore before God, and the Lord Jesus Christ, who shall judge the quick and the dead at his appearing and his kingdom; Preach the word; be instant in season, out of season; reprove, rebuke, exhort with all longsuffering and doctrine. For the time will come when they will not endure sound doctrine; but after their own lusts shall they heap to themselves teachers, having itching ears; And they shall turn away *their* ears from the truth, and shall be turned unto fables. But watch thou in all things, endure afflictions, do the work of an evangelist, make full proof of thy ministry.
>
> 2 Timothy 4:1-5

The Importance of Sound Doctrine

In his article "When Not Seeing is Believing,"[1] Andrew Sullivan, did his best to explain away "the faith which was once delivered to the saints" (Jude 1:3), i.e. the faith that saves, by defining real faith as a smorgasbord of humanistic faiths. This man seems to believe, as do great numbers within professing Christendom, that there are multiple ways to heaven, i.e. multiple faiths that save. According to Mr. Sullivan, there is a real faith that "never experiences a catharsis or 'born-again' conversion" (This despite the Lord's own plain teaching in John 3:1-21 and Paul's in 2 Corinthians 5:17, Ephesians 4:24, and Colossians 3:10.) This humanistic faith treats the Bible as a "moral fable," puts Muhammad on an equal footing with Jesus Christ, and offers the individual a "cafeteria Christianity," i.e. believe what you like, reject what you don't like. In fact, in this man's opinion, "complete religious certainty is...blasphemy."

Mr. Sullivan most likely thinks the Apostle Paul blasphemous in declaring that "I know whom I have believed, and am persuaded that he is able to keep that which I have committed unto him against that day" (1 Timothy 1:12b). And he must be deeply disappointed in the Apostle John's naïveté when he states, "I have written unto you that believe on the name of the Son of God; *that ye may know* that ye have eternal life" (1 John 5:13a, italics added). These two great saints felt that true faith was, indeed, "complete religious certainty." And so do all who have received the everlasting assurance of real, saving faith through the work of God's own Spirit in their life.

Unfortunately, this man's religious unbelief reflects the thinking of a very large segment of professing Christians today. David Kinnaman, the vice president of the Barna Group that conducted the survey on Americans' beliefs concerning Satan, was quoted in the article previously cited as saying, "It's quite a conundrum for many church leaders, and it's not limited to Satan. People tend to pick and choose teachings that feel right and fit. It's sort of a smorgasbord." The article went on to reflect on this "pick and choose your own doctrines" mentality, quoting Kinnaman as declaring, "It is a sign of syncretism–that is, the blending of faith with culture." His conclusion: "the survey shows an American cultural bias toward spiritual optimism–picking to accept teachings about goodness while choosing against believing in evil supernatural beings." He concludes with the obvious observation that "the survey may reflect a wide but shallow faith in America."

In our subject text, Matthew 7:21-23, the Lord is revealing the time when He will unveil the foolishness of this "wide but shallow faith" that characterizes all man-centered religion. When He does, He will vindicate His eternal, holy, and unchanging Word, and fully manifest His sovereign right to rule over all men in all things. At the Great Judgment, He will put all of man's wisdom and blasphemous reasoning aside and draw His final and perfect judgment. On that day, the apparent faith of the "religious lost" will be condemned, and the true believer's saving faith rewarded.

> All the ways of a man *are* clean in his own eyes; but the LORD weigheth the spirits.
>
> Proverbs 16:2

> Be not deceived; God is not mocked: for whatsoever a man soweth, that shall he also reap. For he that soweth to his flesh shall of the flesh reap corruption; but he that soweth to the Spirit shall of the Spirit reap life everlasting.
>
> Galatians 6:7-8

Only Sound Doctrine Produces Saving Faith

Today's lack of interest in and commitment to sound doctrine has bred a complacency regarding the many solemn warnings from our Lord regarding the "last days," despite the fact that it seems He was addressing the very age in which we live. This complacency has resulted in a perversion of the true gospel into another gospel, which pleases man, but misrepresents God.

At the root of this problem is a failure to understand the

true nature of God. As a result, man has diminished God's glory and established a false standard of holiness against which he measures himself, that is, his own righteousness rather than God's. Consequently, the religious-but-lost man foolishly lives his life according to his own carnal reasoning about sin, righteousness, and judgment, rather than according to the truth of God's Word and its holy demands.

As A.W. Tozer eloquently notes in his classic book *The Knowledge of the Holy*:

> Before the Christian Church goes into eclipse anywhere there must first be a corrupting of her simple basic theology. She simply gets a wrong answer to the question, "What is God like?" and goes on from there. Though she may continue to cling to a sound nominal creed, her practical working creed has become false. The masses of her adherents come to believe that God is different from what He actually is; and that is heresy of the most insidious and deadly kind.[2]

In his letter to the Romans, Paul spoke of the true gospel being "the power of God unto salvation to every one that believeth" (Romans 1:16). He goes on immediately to state why salvation is needed and what men need to be saved from.

> For the wrath of God is revealed from heaven against all ungodliness and unrighteousness of men, who hold the truth in unrighteousness; Because that which may be known of God is manifest in them; for God hath showed *it* unto them.
> Romans 1:18-19

In commenting on this passage and its context, D. Martyn Lloyd-Jones emphasized to his listeners the following:

> You notice that the Apostle puts "ungodliness" first, and that in his thinking "unrighteousness" only follows ungodliness. To him the big thing, the important thing, is "ungodliness."
>
> This is particularly important today, for the modern approach in the Church, and obviously in the world, is to say that the real problem is that of unrighteousness and that alone. Ungodliness is not mentioned. The great problem, we are told, is in the problem of man, and particularly the problem of man in society. We are told that the great need today is to reconcile man to man, and that this is the task of the Church ... Someone has summed it up by saying that man's great need is to find a "gracious neighbor," and this is the task before us. And in addition to this, and to that end, we are told that what we need is to be cured of our ills and weaknesses. Sin is regarded as sickness, a disease, of which we need to be cured. But all the time, you notice, it is in terms of man, and man's relationship to man. It does not mention what the Apostle puts first—ungodliness, man in his relationship to God.
>
> That is the essence of this modern attitude ... [But] man's first need is the need of knowing God, of discovering, as Luther put it, "a gracious God," not a gracious neighbor.
>
> This is man's primary need ... As our Lord Himself replied when asked by a lawyer which was the first commandment of all, "Thou shalt

love the Lord thy God with all thy heart, and with all thy soul, and with all thy mind, and with all thy strength; this is the first commandment." "And the second"... is "thou shalt love thy neighbour as thyself" [Mark 12:28:31] But no man will ever "love his neighbor as himself" until he first loves God. He does not know the truth about himself. You cannot love your neighbour as yourself if you do not know the truth about yourself...[3]

Untold millions of professing Christians today don't truly know God, and the fruit of their lives is the evidence of that reality. The gospel they have been taught and in which they have placed their faith is a gospel that reflects a god of man's own design, a god made in the image of man! Being human, man has created in his own mind a humanistic god. The religious-but-lost man's god winks at sin. He is a creator who sets aside his own holiness in the presence of sin lest he appear to be too "judgmental" of his wayward creatures. Unfortunately for man, this god does not exist. Consequently, he cannot save.

To quote Tozer once more, "The vague and tenuous hope that God is too kind to punish the ungodly has become a deadly opiate for the consciences of millions."[4] Yes, as he said, this is a "heresy of the most insidious and deadly kind," a heresy that is leading untold millions to unexpected and eternal damnation.

The Lord *is* slow to anger, and great in power,
[but He] will not at all acquit *the wicked*.
Nahum 1:3

Who Perverted the Love of God?

The Jews of Christ's time had the same perverted view of God's love as do multitudes today. The Lord once told a group of them, "If ye continue in my word, *then* are ye my disciples indeed; And ye shall know the truth, and the truth shall make you free" (John 8:31b-32). Their reaction was immediate, unbelieving, and aggressively defensive: "They answered him, We be Abraham's seed, and were never in bondage to any man: how sayest thou, Ye shall be made free?" (John 8:33).

Their sin had perverted their understanding of the love and character of God! They thought that their covenant relationship with God shielded them from His judgment, His wrath. Their spiritual blindness even kept them from acknowledging their own history! They seemed to have forgotten the four hundred years of slavery in Egypt, their bondage under the Babylonian kingdom, and chastenings too numerous to mention here.

The blinding power of the sin of self-righteousness

is awesome. Its strength lies in man's desire to escape the judgment that his conscience tells him is inevitable. In his attempt to deny the reality of the Great Judgment, his perverted thinking pits God against Himself! He sets God's love, mercy, and kindness in conflict with His holiness, righteousness, and wrath. He, in effect, divides the Godhead, claiming for himself the attributes of God that he finds pleasing and convenient for his self-justification, while denying, or at least diminishing, the attributes of God that disturb or convict him. This is what Tozer was expressing when he said errors in church doctrine and practice result when a church "simply gets a wrong answer to the question, 'What is God like?' and goes on from there."[1]

But God has declared the plain and simple truth of the matter; i.e. His true nature, in no uncertain terms:

> I *am* the LORD, I change not.
>
> Malachi 3:6a

> Jesus Christ the same yesterday, and to day, and for ever.
>
> Hebrews 13:8

If God were to change to any degree, in any way, He would not be God. If he could set aside any of His attributes or emphasize any of His attributes to the diminishing of any other, He would not be God. He has declared "I am the LORD, I change not" (Malachi 3:6) for He is "the Father of lights, with whom is no variableness, neither shadow of turning" (James 1:17).

God's love is neither greater nor less than His holiness, nor are they in any way contradictory. God's mercy is neither greater nor less than His justice, nor are they in any way contradictory. God's grace is neither greater nor less than His wrath, nor are they in any way contradictory.

The religious-but-lost man wants to believe that the cross of Calvary changed God. He wants to believe that because of the cross, God no longer holds man accountable to the same standards He held His people to in the Old Testament, and, consequently, will not exercise His wrath toward his sins in the same way He did towards theirs. He wants to believe the cross was simply a proclamation of God's love, which forgives him for all of his sin. Then, with this proclamation in hand, he wants to go on sinning!

The fact is that the cross of Calvary vindicated God's eternal, that is to say, His past, present, *and* future wrath against sin. It sets before man both blessed hope and utter hopelessness. It offers hope to all who truly trust wholly in the finished work of the Savior who hung on that cross, the sure hope of receiving the benefit of His death, i.e. the righteousness required for eternal life: God's righteousness: "For he hath made him *to be* sin for us, who knew no sin; that we might be made the righteousness of God in him" (2 Corinthians 5:21).

On the other hand, it represents utter hopelessness for those who do not *truly* accept God's Lamb as the *only* and all-sufficient payment for their sins because the wrath of God still rests on them, and He will vindicate His holiness. These will be brought before the bar of God's justice to answer for their own sins and, having rejected God's payment, will be required to pay their own price for rejecting God's way. That price will be personal, eternal death.

Was the cross the proclamation of God's love? Of course it was. But that proclamation is not a license to sin or a declaration that the righteousness of God will be set aside for anyone giving mere mental assent to or superficial acknowledgement of that love.

The cross was the turning point in man's history. And for the true believer who sincerely repents of his sins and places his trust in the Savior slain on the cross of Calvary, it is the turning point in his life. To believe in Jesus Christ as both Lord and Savior is a transforming experience that vitally and practically changes his life and its fruit forever.

Paul had to deal with the same self-righteousness in the Jews in his day that Christ had dealt with during His time on earth. Those he addressed in his Roman letter thought themselves above his exhortations. They felt secure in their covenant relationship with God and considered themselves to be without need for the grace of God that Paul had declared by the authority of God. They saw the need for God's grace to the Gentiles, certainly, but not for themselves. But they were wrong.

In addressing their unholy, self-righteous spirit, Paul attempted to show them its ungodly nature as follows: "Or despisest thou the riches of his goodness and forbearance and longsuffering; not knowing that the goodness of God ... leadeth thee to repentance?" (Romans 2:4).

How could they despise "the riches of his goodness and forbearance and longsuffering" while claiming His blessings as their own? Because their understanding of salvation was not based on the truth. In their spiritual ignorance and personal arrogance, they actually condemned themselves and rejected the salvation they claimed was theirs!

> Brethren, my heart's desire and prayer to God for Israel is, that they might be saved. For I bear them record that they have a zeal of God, but not according to knowledge. For they being ignorant of God's righteousness, and going about to establish their own righteousness, have not submitted themselves unto the righteousness of God.
>
> Romans 10:1-3

How could this happen? How could these who claimed to love God, and be the recipients of His everlasting love, actually despise His ways? They were blinded by their own self-righteousness because their religion was man-centered and self-serving, not God-centered and self-denying.

In bringing the truth of this passage to bear on the modern church, D. Martyn Lloyd-Jones, in essence, answers the question, "How could anyone who is truly saved regard the love and goodness of God in such a way as to hold that it gives us a license to go on sinning?"

> Let me put it to you like this: this view of God is guilty, is it not, of using what it regards as the truth about God to serve its own ends, and I suppose there is no greater insult that we can offer God than that. These people are primarily concerned about going on with the sinful kind of life which appeals to them. So they are unconsciously constructing a god for themselves who will allow

them to do that. They are using God's goodness as a license and a liberty, a cloak and an excuse for their own sin. And that is simply to use God— even God—to serve our own ends.[2]

With this perspective, it is easier to understand the Lord's words in Matthew 7:23, "Depart from me ye that work iniquity." Our Savior later gave this condemnation additional substance in His revelation to John, when He prophetically described the church at Laodicea. This church is given as a type of apostasy in any age but especially of the church that will exist when the Lord returns to earth.

> And unto the angel of the church of the Laodiceans write; These things saith the Amen, the faithful and true witness, the beginning of the creation of God; I know thy works, that thou art neither cold nor hot: I would thou wert cold or hot. So then because thou art lukewarm, and neither cold nor hot, I will spue thee out of my mouth. Because thou sayest, I am rich, and increased with goods, and have need of nothing; and knowest not that thou art wretched, and miserable, and poor, and blind, and naked: I counsel thee to buy of me gold tried in the fire, that thou mayest be rich; and white raiment, that thou mayest be clothed, and *that* the shame of thy nakedness do not appear; and anoint thine eyes with eyesalve, that thou mayest see. As many as I love, I rebuke and chasten: be zealous therefore, and repent.
>
> Revelation 3:14–19

Notice that both the Romans' passage and this passage from the Revelation emphasize repentance. Lloyd-Jones emphasized this as he broke out the key terms of the Roman passage in his subsequent comments.

> Very well, then, that brings us to our last term, which is the term *repentance*..."The goodness of God leadeth thee to repentance"—first. It is the thing he put in the forefront. And you know the whole gospel does the same.
>
> Who is the first preacher in the New Testament? He is John the Baptist. What did he preach? The baptism of repentance for the remission of sins. That is the first note always in gospel preaching. The first business of the preacher of salvation is to call men to repentance.
>
> Look further: it is not only true of John the Baptist, our Lord did the same thing. Read in Mark the account of the beginning of our Lord's ministry and you will find that we are told that he went and preached everywhere that men should repent.
>
> Repentance! You start with it. Obviously you do not see the need of a Saviour unless you have seen yourself as a sinner and in the wrong relationship to God. It must be repentance first, otherwise you are not interested in salvation.[3]

A gospel that does not provide a complete picture of man's sinful nature in contrast to God's perfectly holy nature cannot provoke the sinner to believe "unto salvation" (Romans 1:16). The "belief" that saves is very clearly defined by the Apostle Paul as the fruit of the work of

God's grace that provokes in the true believer both "repentance toward God, and faith toward our Lord Jesus Christ" (Acts 20:21).

Sadly, today's religious-but-lost man doesn't see the need to repent, for he does not view sin as an offense against the perfectly holy God who is bound by His own character to judge all offenses according to the standard of His own infinite righteousness. Rather, he views sin as simply the weakness of man that gives God an occasion to manifest His grace to the sinner. This false doctrine is being perpetuated throughout the world despite the Bible's direct warning against adopting such a perverted view of God's grace: "What shall we say then? Shall we continue in sin, that grace may abound? God forbid. How shall we, that are dead to sin, live any longer therein?" (Romans 6:1-2).

As a result of its incorrect views of God's holiness, sin, and the cross, man-centered religion preaches a message that deceives unregenerate man. It presents a gospel that declares that the love of God has provided an excuse for his sins rather than a just and infinitely valuable payment for his deliverance from *both* the penalty *and* the dominion of sin. Instead of serving as a provocation to true holiness as God commands, this false gospel serves as the means for "Christianizing" unholiness.

In the August 28, 2006 issue of his online blog, Albert Mohler, President of Southern Theological Seminary in Louisville, Kentucky, wrote this:

> The approach of many churches—and preachers—has been to present helpful and practical mes-

sages, often with generalized Christian content, but without any clear presentation of the Gospel or call to decision and accountability to the text or to the claims of Christ. The apostles should be our model here, consistently preaching the death, burial, and resurrection of Jesus Christ. Of course, in order for the Gospel to make sense, authentic preaching must also deal honestly with the reality of human sin, and must do so with a candor equal to that of the biblical text. All this presents the preacher with some significant challenges in our age of "sensitivities." But in the end, preaching devoid of this content—preaching that evades the biblical text and biblical truth—falls short of anything we can rightly call *Christian* preaching.[4]

Friend, if what Mohler says is true (and I believe it is), and if the Bible is true when it tells us that we are saved by grace through faith (and it is), and if that faith comes by hearing the Word of God (and it does), then, if multitudes are not under the sound of truly Christ-centered preaching that is faithful to the sound doctrines of the holy scriptures, how can they be taught the true faith of Christ? And if they are never taught the true faith of Christ, how can they exercise real faith? And if they cannot exercise real faith, how can they be saved?

When one takes God out of his knowledge, he has no truth to stand on. As a consequence, he becomes foolish and blind to his disobedience to God, even calling "evil good, and good evil."[5] No wonder there will be multitudes standing before God's judgment seat expecting entrance into heaven when, according to Jesus Christ, their eternal residence will be hell!

For a better understanding of the true nature of God the following is recommended:

Made In Our Image, Steven J. Lawson, Multnomah Publishers, Inc., Sisters, OR

Man-Centered Religion's Definition of a Christian

The people the Lord described in Matthew 7:21-23 are convinced they are His disciples, i.e. Christians. Yet He will condemn them to hell because their "Christianity," their faith, is faulty. Their view of what it means to be a Christian is fatally wrong because it is based on man's definition, not God's.

A Christian, according to *Merriam-Webster* is "an adherent of Christianity." But what does it mean to be an "adherent," and what is meant by "Christianity?"

This same dictionary defines *adherent* in a two-fold way: "1: to give support: maintain loyalty; or 2: to stick fast: Cling." It also defines Christianity as "the religion derived from Jesus Christ, based on the Bible as sacred scripture, and professed by Christians." Bringing these together, our current culture's definition of a Christian, at least according to this source, would be: "Anyone who professes to loyally support the religion derived from Jesus Christ based on the Bible as sacred scripture."

This does seem to represent the understanding of the vast majority of people today. But, while there is certainly truth in this definition, it falls far short of "the faith once delivered to the saints" (Jude 1:3) and taught by God's holy Word. In fact, this definition is even inconsistent with the actual beliefs of many today who consider themselves to be "Christians."

Mormonism, for example, is known formally as "The Church of Jesus Christ of Latter-Day Saints," which implies it has some association with historical Christianity. But the Jesus Mormons worship is definitely *not* the Jesus of the Bible. Jehovah's Witnesses are also associated with the Christian faith by some, yet they do *not* worship the Jesus of the Bible either. The same can be said of the Seventh Day Adventists and Christian Scientists.

How is it possible to say that adherents of these faiths are not real Christians? Without going into a detailed analysis of their theology that would prove this beyond a shadow of a doubt, the "bottom line" is that each of these groups shares one belief, actually an *un*belief, which absolutely disqualifies them from being real Christians. They deny the virgin birth of Jesus. Not believing that Jesus was God incarnate, i.e. God became fully man but without sin, none of these can declare with the Apostle Thomas, "My Lord and my God" (John 20:28). Nor can they believe the foundational truths necessary for salvation by faith in Jesus Christ as declared by the Apostle John:

> In the beginning was the Word, and the Word was with God, and the Word was God. The same was in the beginning with God. All things were made

> by him; and without him was not any thing made
> that was made. In him was life; and the life was
> the light of men ... and the Word was made flesh,
> and dwelt among us, (and we beheld his glory, the
> glory as of the only begotten of the Father,) full of
> grace and truth.
>
> John 1:1-4, 14

So, having fully declared their unbelief in the doctrine of the incarnation and virgin birth of Jesus Christ, they cannot be counted among the believers described by John in the same passage:

> But as many as received him, to them gave he
> power to become the sons of God, *even* to them
> that believe on his name: Which were born, not of
> blood, nor of the will of the flesh, nor of the will of
> man, but of God.
>
> John 1:12-13

To put it plainly, the Jesus these worship is "another Jesus."[1] As a result, the gospel they preach is "another gospel" (Galatians 1:6-9), a perverted gospel that cannot save and must be rejected by all real Christians who would be faithful witnesses of the true gospel, the gospel of God's salvation offered only through the finished work of His eternal and only Son, Jesus Christ.[2]

Strong language? Yes. Uncomfortable to declare? Yes. But God's Word is truth, and it expressly teaches that the preaching of any gospel other than the gospel of the grace of God in Christ Jesus as fully revealed and explained in the epistles to the church is strictly forbidden.

> I marvel that ye are so soon removed from him that called you into the grace of Christ unto another gospel: Which is not another; but there be some that trouble you, and would pervert the gospel of Christ. But though we, or an angel from heaven, preach any other gospel unto you than that which we have preached unto you, let him be accursed. As we said before, so say I now again, If any *man* preach any other gospel unto you than that ye have received, let him be accursed. For do I now persuade men, or God? Or do I seek to please men? For if I yet pleased men, I should not be the servant of Christ. But I certify you, brethren, that the gospel which was preached of me is not after man.
>
> Galatians 1:6-11

So, if the Bible is true (and it is), and if true Christianity is based on its teachings "as sacred scripture" (and it is), then the followers of these religions and others that espouse equally damning errors are *not* Christians, even by Webster's very generic definition.

The problem with man's definition of a Christian is that it is man-centered not Christ-centered. Consequently, man's definition results in a belief system that is man-directed. Man-centered and man-directed religion points man to himself. It encourages him to lean on his own strength to "adhere" to a faith, to trust that his own work is sufficient to please God.

But true Christianity is fully Christ-centered and God-directed. It sets aside all of man's works as being no better than "filthy rags" (Isaiah 64:6), completely inadequate to save him. It points man to the Savior, Jesus Christ, as his only but all-sufficient and wholly available hope. It is a salvation provided to the believer through the will and work of God by grace alone, apart from any of man's religious works or any other agencies.

The Savior Himself said:

> I am the way, the truth, and the life: no man cometh unto the Father, but by me.
>
> John 14:6

> All that the Father giveth me shall come to me; and him that cometh to me I will in no wise cast out. For I came down from heaven, not to do mine own will, but the will of him that sent me. And this is the Father's will which hath sent me, that of all which he hath given me I should lose nothing, but should raise it up again at the last day. And this is the will of him that sent me, that every one which seeth the Son, and believeth on him, may have everlasting life: and I will raise him up at the last day.
>
> John 6:37-40

> No man can come to me, except the Father which hath sent me draw him: and I will raise him up at the last day.
>
> John 6:44

When Jesus's disciples asked Him to teach them about the end times and his promise to establish His throne on earth, Jesus told them that it would be a time when many very attractive false gospels would abound. He taught that these gospels would be very powerful, extremely compelling to the human mind, and so bewitching that it would be very easy to be deceived by them were it not for the attention of the Holy Spirit for His elect.

> Then if any man shall say unto you, Lo, here *is* Christ, or there; believe *it* not. For there shall arise false Christs, and false prophets, and shall show great signs and wonders; insomuch that, if *it were* possible, they shall deceive the very elect. Behold, I have told you before.
>
> Matthew 24:23-25

The reference here to earlier warnings, "I have told you before," is a direct reference to His teachings recorded in Matthew 7:21-23 and its context, Matthew 13:18-23 (parable of the sower), Matthew 13:36-43 (parable of the tares among the wheat), and Matthew 13:47-50 (parable of the net) in which Jesus warned in no uncertain terms of the coming Day of Judgment. Christ's determination to make the reality of the Judgment Day and hell known to everyone who had ears to hear Him is a measure of His love, for He is "not willing that any should perish, but that all should come to repentance" (2 Peter 3:9b).

The Christian's love for mankind must mirror his Lord's. In this age when great numbers of sincere people are being deceived into trusting in their own good works through the erroneous teachings of man-centered religion, he must be a faithful witness. He must determine to diligently watch for and charitably expose the false teachings that offer man a false hope and damn him to hell. He must faithfully declare the true gospel of the grace of God in Jesus Christ that offers eternal salvation to everyone who comes to Jesus Christ by faith alone. Manifesting the character of his Savior, he must be "Faithful and True" (Revelation 19:11) in presenting "all the counsel of God" (Acts 20:27), His view of sin not man's, His way of salvation not man's. He, in short, must be a faithful and courageous ambassador for "Christ, the Saviour of the world" (John 4:42b).

The God of Man-Centered Religion

All that has been shared thus far should make very clear the nature of the real problem today; namely, that there is a "Christianity" being preached today that exalts the god of self rather than the God of sacrifice, the God of true salvation. The righteousness of the one and only true and holy God has been replaced by man's *self*-righteousness. The pursuit of God's glory has been set aside in favor of the pursuit of man-defined *self*-esteem. Salvation has been redefined as various forms of *self*-worship. Rather than coming humbly to the "true Light" (John 1:9), Jesus Christ, to find the truth of God, men are encouraged to pursue *self*-ordained journeys of *self*-enlightenment. And, rather than setting one's "affection on things above" (Colossians 3:1), today's religious teachers promote various forms of the attractive but erroneous secular doctrine of "What the mind can conceive and believe, it can achieve."

A.W. Tozer brings sober and holy perspective to this gospel of self as he comments on the self-existence of God.

A more positive assertion of selfhood could not be imagined than those words of God to Moses, I AM THAT I AM. Everything God is, everything that is God, is set forth in that unqualified declaration of independent being. Yet in God, self is not sin, but the quintessence of all possible goodness, holiness, and truth.

The natural man is a sinner because and only because he challenges God's selfhood in relation to his own. In all else he may willingly accept the sovereignty of God; in his own life he rejects it. For him, God's dominion ends where his begins. For him, self becomes Self, and in this he unconsciously imitates Lucifer, that fallen son of the morning who said in his heart, "I will ascend into heaven, I will exalt my throne above the stars of God … I will be like the most High."

Yet, so subtle is self that scarcely anyone is conscious of its presence. Because man is a rebel, he is unaware that he is one. His constant assertion of self, as far as he thinks of it at all, appears to him a perfectly normal thing. He is willing to share himself, sometimes even to sacrifice himself for a desired end, but never to dethrone himself. No matter how far down the scale of social acceptance he may slide, he is still in his own eyes, a king on a throne, and no one, not even God, can take that throne from him.[1]

This sin of self-enthronement was illustrated graphically when the Lord rebuked His people through the prophet Isaiah. In His complaint against His people's wickedness, He had declared, "For thus saith the LORD that created the heavens; God himself that formed the earth and made it; he hath established it, he created it not in vain, he formed it to be inhabited: I *am* the LORD; and *there is* none else" (Isaiah 45:18). Having stated the truth of His absolute supremacy and sovereignty, He rebuked His chosen nation because "thou hast trusted in thy wickedness: thou hast said, None seeth me. Thy wisdom and thy knowledge, it hath perverted thee; and thou hast said in thine heart, I *am*, and none else beside me" (Isaiah 47:10).

Without realizing it, God's people had broken the very first commandment He had given them through Moses: "Thou shalt have no other gods before me" (Exodus 20:3). I AM is God's name, the name He had revealed to Moses at the burning bush when He called him to lead His people out of Egypt into the land He had promised their forefathers.[2] By leaning on their own understanding and thereby exalting their own will over God's, they had rejected God's right to rule their life and had committed themselves to their own self-rule. They had dethroned God and become their own god. "Self" had become, in principle and practice, their "I AM."

The Lord warns us of this god of self through the Apostle Paul's final instructions to the young minister Timothy.

> This know also, that in the last days perilous times shall come. For men shall be lovers of *their own selves*...more than lovers of God; having a form of godliness, but denying the power thereof: from such turn away.
>
> 2 Timothy 3:1-2 (italics added)

Today, religious-but-lost humanity bases its faith on the teachings of men rather than the Word of God, and submits to the rule of self rather than the sovereign rule of God. Having accepted some form of self-centered faith that they have been taught by the modern church or some other religious organization, they rightly view themselves as "believers." Yet they remain unsaved because what they believe is wrong.

Tragic? Yes. Unexpected? No.

Man-centered religion ruled by the god of self has been around as long as man. The Lord condemned His people for this through the prophets Isaiah and Ezekiel:

> Wherefore the Lord said, Forasmuch as this people draw near *me* with their mouth, and with their lips do honour me, but have removed their heart far from me, and their fear toward me is taught by the precept of men: Therefore, behold, I will proceed to do a marvelous work among this people, *even* a marvelous work and a wonder: for the wisdom of their wise *men* shall perish, and the understanding of their prudent *men* shall be hid.
>
> Isaiah 29:13

> And they come unto thee as the people cometh, and they sit before thee *as* my people, and they hear thy words, but they will not do them: for with their mouth they shew much love, *but* their heart goeth after their covetousness.
>
> Ezekiel 33:31

In other words, they had formed a man-centered religion headed by a god of their own design, formed according to their own precepts and understandings. Though they believed themselves to be serving God, they were serving the false god of self with great zeal for personal gain. In love, God warned them very plainly that their worship was a denial of His wisdom and grace, and a rebellion against His sovereign rule against which He would bring divine judgment.

Lest someone think, *Oh, those are just Old Testament prophecies; they are not applicable to us today*, the Lord Jesus Christ referred directly to the Isaiah passage above when addressing the religious hypocrites of His time on earth, proving the perpetual nature of this sin as well as the unchanging view of God toward it:

> Thus have ye made the commandment of God of none effect by your tradition. *Ye* hypocrites, well did Esaias prophesy of you, saying, This people draweth nigh unto me with their mouth, and honoureth me with *their* lips; but their heart is far from me. But in vain they do worship me, teaching *for* doctrines the commandments of men.
>
> Matthew 15:6-9

Paul reaffirmed the danger of man-centered religion in his last pastoral letter to Timothy:

> I charge *thee* therefore before God, and the Lord Jesus Christ, who shall judge the quick and the dead at his appearing and his kingdom; Preach the

word; be instant in season, out of season; reprove, rebuke, exhort with all longsuffering and doctrine. For the time will come when they will not endure sound doctrine; but after their own lusts shall they heap to themselves teachers, having itching ears; And they shall turn away *their* ears from the truth, and shall be turned unto fables.

2 Timothy 4:1-4

Finally, in His Revelation to John, the Lord condemned the church at Laodicea, which represents erroneous, humanistic religion of any age, for the same sin:

I know thy works, that thou art neither cold nor hot: I would thou wert cold or hot. So then because thou art lukewarm [note: This is the temperature of the flesh, that is, carnal], and neither cold nor hot, I will spue thee out of my mouth. Because thou sayest, I am rich, and increased with goods, and have need of nothing [note: religious man's opinion of himself]; and knowest not that thou art wretched, and miserable, and poor, and blind, and naked [note: God's opinion of religious man]: I counsel thee to buy of me gold tried in the fire, that thou mayest be rich; and white raiment, that thou mayest be clothed, and *that* the shame of thy nakedness do not appear; and anoint thine eyes with eyesalve, that thou mayest see. As many as I love, I rebuke and chasten: be zealous therefore, and repent.

Revelation 3:15-19

Will just "any" faith secure eternal life in heaven? No.

The age of the great Reformation followed what historians once called the Dark Ages. It could be argued that there was never a time in history when mankind was, in relative terms, more superstitious, immoral, and ignorant of God and His ways. That spiritual ignorance continued into the Reformation period due to the refusal of the Roman Catholic Church to allow the publication and distribution of the Word of God to the "common man." Because of this, individuals who lived in that time were ignorant of the true way of salvation yet died believing they had been saved because of their blind faith in and obedience to the sacraments and traditions they had been taught. Religious? Yes. Believers? Yes ... in the works they were taught by their church. Saved?

The following testimony is from one whose unique life exposed him to both sides of religion, the true, which teaches that salvation is by grace alone through faith alone in Jesus Christ alone, and the false, which teaches that man is saved by faith plus works of some kind. This man forsook the Word of God alone as the source of all truth, and placed his trust instead in the teachings and traditions of his church and his own works. Facing death, he came to realize his horrible error.

> Francis Spira was a Venetian lawyer, an Italian of wealth, learning and eloquence who, attracted by the fame of Martin Luther and the principles of the Reformation, became a preacher [at least in form]. For six years, he proclaimed the evangelical doctrines represented by the Reformation. The

persecutions of the time that were directed against Christians frightened him, and he [was revealed to be] an apostate [i.e. someone who had, at some point in his life, manifested the appearance of being a true believer, but who had never actually been saved]. In the presence of two thousand people he recanted and acknowledged once more the Roman Catholic doctrines. As soon as this public recantation was over, Spira took seriously ill and implored someone to kill him. Friends came to bid him farewell and were horrified at his cursing and blasphemy against God. In his last hour he confessed…

I have denied Christ voluntarily and against my convictions. I feel that He hardens me, and will allow me no hope. It is a fearful thing to fall into the hands of the living God! I feel the weight of His wrath burning like the pains of hell within me. I am one of those whom God has threatened to tear asunder.

Oh, the cursed day! Would I had never been at Venice. I am like the rich man, who though he was in hell, was anxious that his brethren should escape torment. Judas, after betraying his Master, was compelled to own his sin and to declare the innocence of Christ, and it is neither new nor singular that I do the same. The mercy of Christ is a strong rampart against the wrath of God; but I have demolished that bulwark with my own hands.

Take heed of relying on that faith which works not a holy and unblameable life worthy of a believer. It will fail. I have tried. I presumed I had the right faith. I preached it to others. I had all places in Scripture in memory that might support it. I thought myself sure, and in the meantime lived impiously and carelessly. Now the judgment of God hath overtaken me, not to correction, but to damnation.[3]

God is a jealous God. He will not share His throne with anyone or any thing. Rather, He will bring judgment on anyone who attempts, knowingly or unknowingly, to dethrone Him. He alone is sovereign and supreme. Man is commanded throughout His Holy Word to bow down in honor to Him as such. The first step to salvation, then, is to recognize and reject the deceitfulness of the sinful god of self and sincerely and fully submit to the true and sovereign living God. The god of self damns, but the everlasting and gracious God of heaven and earth saves.

Works That Deceive and the One Work That Saves

A closer look at Matthew 7:21-23 will provide needed insight into the works that deceived these religious-but-lost individuals: "Many will say to me in that day, Lord, Lord, have we not prophesied in thy name? and in thy name have cast out devils? And in thy name done many wonderful works?" (Matthew 7:22)

The Lord does not reject their claims. The fact that they produced these works is not at issue. What is at issue are their source and their value. Christ will address both matters by placing His divine seal of *dis*approval on all of them, rejecting them as not being from Him and, there-fore, of no value. He will conclude that they are, in fact, not good works but "iniquity," i.e., wickedness.

The Bible plainly teaches that man is not saved by works, any works. In fact, if one attempts to please God with his works, he is deceived and brings on him-self increasing condemnation, for in attempting to save himself he is rejecting God's sacrifice for salvation, Jesus

Christ, the Lamb of God who died to take away the sins of the world. He is, in effect, offering himself as the sacrifice for his own sins. What an immeasurable offense this is to the holy and all gracious God.

What are the works that deceive these religious-but-lost individuals despite the very plain teachings of God's Holy Word?

Works That Deceive

1.   They "prophesied."

The Strong's Greek Dictionary's definition for the word from which this is translated is "to foretell events, divine, speak under inspiration, exercise the prophetic office." Today, this may be combined with what is called "speaking in tongues," and other superficial, sensual, and "showy" behavior to impress listeners. Those who claim to have this gift represent to their followers that their proclamations are from God so that they are not confined in their teachings to the Word of God. In other words, they claim that their "visions" are an addition to the Bible's teachings.

Two passages come immediately to mind that should be sufficient for the true Christian to see the error behind such claims:

> For I testify unto every man that heareth the words of the prophecy of this book, If any man shall add unto these things, God shall add unto him the plagues that are written in this book: And if any man shall take away from the words of the book of

this prophecy, God shall take away his part out of the book of life, and out of the holy city, and *from* the things which are written in this book.

Revelation 22:18-19

And if thou say in thine heart, How shall we know the word which the Lord hath not spoken? When a prophet speaketh in the name of the Lord, if the thing follow not, nor come to pass, that *is* the thing which the Lord hath not spoken, *but* the prophet hath spoken it presumptuously: thou shalt not be afraid of him.

Deuteronomy 18:21-22

The Bible is complete. There are no "extra-biblical" revelations being received from God today. In fact, those who would "add to" or "take away from" God's Word come under the curse of the Revelation passage above.

There is a sure test of whether a so-called prophet is truly sent by God or is a false prophet: the prophecies of true prophets are *always* fulfilled. The prophecies of false prophets fail. In describing to His disciples the false prophets who would be among these religious-but-lost individuals, the Lord warned: "Beware of false prophets, which come to you in sheep's clothing, but inwardly they are ravening wolves. Ye shall know them by their fruits" (Matthew 7:15-16a).

On January 1, 1990, [Benny] Hinn attempted to delude devotees into believing that God spoke to him and revealed the fate of Castro in Cuba and homosexuals in America: "The Spirit tells me Fidel Castro will die in the '90s." Not only so, asserted Hinn, but "he will not stay in power."...Regarding the homosexual community in America, Hinn alleged the Almighty revealed to him both the timing and the means of their demise. Said Hinn, "The Lord also tells me to tell you in the mid-90s, about '94, '95, on later than that, God will destroy the homosexual community of America. But He will not destroy it with what many minds have thought Him to be [sic]. He will destroy it with fire."

In 1993, Hinn ponfiticated that because Jesus promised that He would return within a generation of Israel's restoration in 1948 and because a generation was "51.4" years—six years remained before Christ would come back to rapture His saints. Seven years later, on March 29, 2000, Hinn predicted Jesus would "appear physically in one of our crusades in the next few months." According to Hinn, the Lord had spoken to the now-deceased Ruth Heflin, saying, "Tell Benny I'm going to appear physically on the platform in his meeting."

Obviously, none of these prophecies has been fulfilled. When someone declares that he (or she) has received a so-called revelation or prophecy from God, and that prophecy does not come to pass, that person is a false prophet by definition. Further, as the Word says, we are not to be "afraid of him." The Strong's Hebrew dictionary defines the word from which *afraid* is translated as meaning "properly, to turn aside from the road (for lodging or any other purpose), i.e. sojourn (as a guest); also to shrink, fear (as in a strange place); also to gather for hostility (as afraid)." In other words, men should neither go out of their way to see or hear such nonsense, nor should they be afraid of any "power" that these self-proclaimed prophets claim to possess. Whatever power they have is not of the Lord, and all powers are subject to Christ in whom the real Christian lives and safely abides.[2]

> Thus saith the LORD of hosts, Hearken not unto the words of the prophets that prophesy unto you: they make you vain: they speak a vision of their own heart, *and* not out of the mouth of the LORD ... Behold, I *am* against them that prophesy false dreams, saith the LORD, and do tell them, and cause my people to err by their lies, and by their lightness; yet I sent them not, nor commanded them: therefore they shall not profit this people at all, saith the LORD.
>
> Jeremiah 23:16, 32

Conclusion: False prophets do not speak the truth. While they may impress unregenerate men, their message cannot save them. Those who cling to the hope that some external "gift," whether theirs or another's, is their ticket to heaven are deceived.

2. They "cast out devils."

Is this possible? Yes it is, but it is not necessarily a sign of the Lord's work. The Lord's detractors gave some useful perspective on this when they attacked His own power over devils. "And the scribes which came down from Jerusalem said, He hath Beelzebub, and by the prince of the devils casteth he out devils" (Matthew 3:22).

Of course, the Lord did not do His works by the power of Satan (Beelzebub) but by His own power. However, Satan does have the power to do many impressive works in his own realm (he is "the god of this world"—2 Corinthians 4:4) within the constraints of God's sovereign reign and eternal purposes. Satan had the ability to empower the sorcerers of Egypt to imitate the miracles God worked through Aaron as they attempted to discredit God's messengers. There is no reason to believe that his power is diminished to any degree in this present age. In fact, we know from the Word that he is very active within the church itself, both from the Lord's teaching of the parable of the tares[3] and Paul's warning to the church at Corinth, which is still applicable.

> For such *are* false apostles, deceitful workers, transforming themselves into the apostles of Christ. And no marvel; for Satan himself is transformed into an angel of light. Therefore *it is* no great thing if his ministers also be transformed as the ministers of righteousness; whose end shall be according to their works.
>
> 2 Corinthians 11:13-15

Conclusion: Some of the most impressive religious works being manifested today may be of Satan, not the Lord. Man is saved by faith, not sight. None of man's works can save, but there are many works that can deceive a person into placing his trust in a false hope so that he can't be saved. This is the intent of the enemy, who would keep all men blind to their real need.

> But if our gospel be hid, it is hid to them that are lost: In whom the god of this world hath blinded the minds of them which believe not, lest the light of the glorious gospel of Christ, who is the image of God, should shine unto them.
>
> 2 Corinthians 4:3-4

3. They did many "wonderful works."

If one confines his thinking to just the English translation here, he will most likely think of these works as simply acts of kindness: caring for the sick, providing for the poor, visiting the shut-ins, etc. While these kinds of ministries are almost certainly associated with these works, they are not the primary "claim to fame" these individuals present to the Lord.

Again the Strong's Greek Dictionary is useful. Its definition of the "wonderful works" these people have tied their hope to is "force (literally or figuratively); specially, miraculous power (usually by implication, a miracle itself)." No wonder these people will be so surprised with the Lord's condemnation. They had worked "miracles" in the name of Christ during their lives (at least in their eyes).

Is this possible? Yes. The sorcerers of Egypt worked miracles. Satan is the god of this world. He has the power to control and manipulate many things. If his ministers can be "transformed as the ministers of righteousness," even though they are in fact ministers of sin and destruction, why should it seem impossible that they can also be used to manifest miraculous powers within his realm to enhance his deceits so as to damn gullible, unregenerate men? The Lord does not condemn their representation that they worked miracles. He simply condemns *all* their works, even their miracles, as being "iniquity."

On the other hand, many of what people today define as "miracles" have been proven to be gross frauds and deceits. Consider how many news programs have been dedicated to exposing the false claims of miracles that have been made by the many charlatans who have dominated cable TV's religious channels. These exposés have proven beyond any doubt that things are not always as they appear to be.

> Network television has sounded its own warnings about [Robert] Tilton. The prayer requests that Tilton promises he will personally pray over all too often end up in garbage dumpsters, as ABC's *PrimeTime Live* cameras have demonstrated.[4]

Conclusion: Miracles may impress man, but they do not impress God unless He is their originator. Miracles are not an evidence of salvation. Even real miracles cannot save.

I have included specific references to the Word of Faith or Faith Movement because I share the goal expressed by the author of *Christianity In Crisis—21st Century* in the introduction to his excellent, meticulously documented book.

Finally, I want to clearly demonstrate to outside observers that the Faith movement does not represent biblical Christianity. In the past few months multiple Faith teachers have been exposed in the national media for questionable beliefs and practices, and I want to cogently communicate that the Faith movement does not represent the historic Christian faith.[5]

The One Work That Saves

The Bible teaches us that there is only one work that saves, only one way to receive eternal life with God in heaven. To illustrate this, Jesus concluded His lesson in Matthew 7 with the story most Christians associate with one of their earliest childhood Sunday school lessons: the wise man and the foolish man.

> Therefore whosoever heareth these sayings of mine, and doeth them, I will liken him unto a wise man, which built his house upon a rock: And the rain descended, and the floods came, and the winds blew, and beat upon that house; and it fell not: for it was founded upon a rock. And every one that heareth these sayings of mine, and doeth them not, shall be likened unto a foolish man, which built his house upon the sand: And the rain descended, and the floods came, and the winds blew, and beat upon that house; and it fell: and great was the fall of it.
>
> Matthew 7:24-27

Everyone is building a "house," and everyone has the choice of placing his house on one of two foundations: sand or rock. Regardless of which foundation he chooses, his house is going to be tested by strong storms. If he places his house on the rock foundation, it will stand up to all tests because the rock foundation is sure, steadfast, and immovable. But the house placed on the sand will be destroyed because it doesn't have a sound foundation. To use the world's terms, it is a "house of cards," a structure without strength. It is just a matter of time before it falls. But this will not be known until the great storm comes.

In a nutshell, the "house" is man's hope of eternal life. The hope of the one who has placed his trust in the Rock of salvation, Jesus Christ, will not fail. His hope is sure. But the hope of foolish religious-but-lost individuals who place their hope on the shifting sands of human reason and man's good works will ultimately fail. The lesson could not be more straightforward.

> According to the grace of God which is given unto me, as a wise masterbuilder, I have laid the foundation, and another buildeth thereon. But let every man take heed how he buildeth thereupon. For other foundation can no man lay than that is laid, which is Jesus Christ.
>
> 1 Corinthians 3:10-11

So here is the truth of the matter. Though multitudes "name the name of Christ," i.e. call themselves Christians, a very large number of these have built their hope on the wrong foundation. And because they have attached their hope to human goodness, good works, and sensual experiences rather than to the sure hope of the substitutionary sacrifice of Jesus Christ for their sins, on the Day of Judgment they will be condemned, rejected by the very One they thought was their Savior! Man's works, whatever they may be, cannot save. Only one work saves: "Jesus answered and said unto them, This is the work of God, that ye believe on him whom he hath sent" (John 6:29).

When one is saved, it is because God has brought the sinner to see and do this work of faith, i.e. to truly believe on the Lord Jesus Christ. He does this through the process of conviction that every born-again believer experiences. It is through this work of love that God shines the light of His Word into the sinner's heart and removes his spiritual blindness[6] so that the Holy Spirit may convince him of three things that one must believe to be saved: (1) the reality of personal sin that is rooted in his very nature, which, if not removed, will bring eternal death, (2) the absence of any personal righteousness that would satisfy God as an offering for the payment for his sin, and (3) the fact of God in His infinite love and wisdom laying the penalty for his sins on His own Son, the perfectly righteous Lamb of God, Jesus Christ, so that he may be saved from eternal death to eternal life by placing his faith in Christ's perfect, once-for-all cross work. "For he hath made him *to be* sin for us, who knew no sin; that we might be made the righteousness of God in him" (2 Corinthians 5:21).

In other words, salvation is by God's grace alone through faith in Jesus Christ alone. Any addition to these three fundamentals of the Christian faith results in the formation of "another gospel" that cannot save.[7]

> God commendeth his love toward us, in that, while we were yet sinners, Christ died for us.
>
> Romans 5:8

> For by grace are ye saved through faith; and that not of yourselves: *it is* the gift of God: Not of works, lest any man should boast.
>
> Ephesians 2:8-9

> But the righteousness which is of faith speaketh on this wise, Say not in thine heart, Who shall ascend into heaven? (that is, to bring Christ down *from above*) Or, Who shall descend into the deep? (that is, to bring up Christ again from the dead.) But what saith it? The word is nigh thee, *even* in thy mouth, and in thy heart: that is, the word of faith, which we preach; That if thou shalt confess with thy mouth the Lord Jesus, and shalt believe in thine heart that God hath raised him from the dead, thou shalt be saved. For with the heart man believeth unto righteousness; and with the mouth confession is made unto salvation. For the scripture saith, Whosoever believeth on him shall not be ashamed.
>
> Romans 10:6-11

Perhaps these words from the wonderful old hymn[8] say it best:

Not the labor of my hands
Can fulfill Thy law's demands;
Could my zeal no respite know,
Could my tears forever flow,
All for sin could not atone;
Thou must save, and Thou alone.

For a Scripture-based understanding of the charismatic movement and the gross errors of the Word of Faith or Faith movement whose theology is often labeled "Name It and Claim It" and/or "Force of Faith," the following are highly recommended.

Charismatic Chaos, John MacArthur, Jr., Zondervan Publishing House, Grand Rapids, MI

Christianity In Crisis–21st Century, Hank Hanegraaff, Thomas Nelson, Nashville, TN

A Real Christian Believes in the Real Jesus Christ

Are there multiple ways to get to heaven? Not according to the Bible. Is any religion "good enough?" Not according to the Bible. Is anyone who claims the name of Jesus and calls Him "Lord" a real Christian? Not according to Jesus!

But if you truly believe that the Bible is the Word of God, understanding who is a real Christian is as easy as "ABC."

A. The Bible clearly declares that Jesus is the Christ.

B. The Bible clearly teaches that faith in Jesus is the only way to God.

C. Only those, then, who have placed saving faith in the biblical Jesus are true Christians and will go to heaven.

Put simply, a real Christian is one who rests his faith entirely on the finished, substitutionary, and wholly sufficient cross work of the Jesus of the Bible.

Who, then, is the Jesus of the Bible who is the only Savior of the world?

1. He is the eternal Son, the Lamb of God, who was ordained to die for the sin of mankind before the world was created.

> The next day John seeth Jesus coming unto him, and saith, Behold the Lamb of God, which taketh away the sin of the world.
>
> John 1:29

> And all that dwell upon the earth shall worship him, whose names are not written in the book of life of the Lamb slain from the foundation of the world.
>
> Romans 13:8

2. He is the Son of God who became a man when the Virgin Mary conceived Him by the Holy Spirit in order that He might become the sin offering for all mankind.

> Now the birth of Jesus Christ was on this wise: When as his mother Mary was espoused to Joseph, before they came together, she was found with child of the Holy Ghost. Then Joseph her husband, being a just *man*, and not willing to make her a publick example, was minded to put her away privily. But while he thought on these things, behold, the angel of the Lord appeared unto him in a dream, saying, Joseph, thou son of David, fear not to take unto thee Mary thy wife: for that which is con-

ceived in her is of the Holy Ghost. And she shall bring forth a son, and thou shalt call his name Jesus: for he shall save his people from their sins. Now all this was done, that it might be fulfilled which was spoken of the Lord by the prophet, saying, Behold, a virgin shall be with child, and shall bring forth a son, and they shall call his name Emmanuel, which being interpreted is, God with us.

Matthew 1:18-23

3. He is the Son of man who was crucified on the cross of Calvary for mankind's sins according to the predetermined will of God as depicted in the gospels. Without His sacrificial, vicarious death, the salvation of man would not have been possible; His life on earth would have accomplished nothing of eternal value.

Saying, The Son of man must suffer many things, and be rejected of the elders and chief priests and scribes, and be slain, and be raised the third day...Let these sayings sink down into your ears: for the Son of man shall be delivered into the hands of men.

Luke 9:22, 44

Ye men of Israel, hear these words; Jesus of Nazareth, a man approved of God among we by miracles and wonders and signs, which God did by him in the midst of we, as ye yourselves also know: Him, being delivered by the determinate counsel and foreknowledge of God, ye have taken, and by wicked hands have crucified and slain.

Acts 2:22-23

Without shedding of blood is no remission. *It was* therefore necessary that the patterns of things in the heavens should be purified with these; but the heavenly things themselves with better sacrifices than these. For Christ is not entered into the holy places made with hands, *which are* the figures of the true; but into heaven itself, now to appear in the presence of God for us: Nor yet that he should offer himself often, as the high priest entereth into the holy place every year with blood of others; For then must he often have suffered since the foundation of the world: but now once in the end of the world hath he appeared to put away sin by the sacrifice of himself.

Hebrews 9:22-26

But as he which hath called you is holy, so be ye holy in all manner of conversation; Because it is written, Be ye holy; for I am holy. And if ye call on the Father, who without respect of persons judgeth according to every man's work, pass the time of your sojourning *here* in fear: Forasmuch as ye know that ye were not redeemed with corruptible things, *as* silver and gold, from your vain conversation *received* by tradition from your fathers; But with the precious blood of Christ, as of a lamb without blemish and without spot: Who verily was foreordained before the foundation of the world, but was manifest in these last times for we, Who by him do believe in God, that raised him up from the dead, and gave him glory; that your faith and hope might be in God.

1 Peter 1:15-21

For he hath made him *to be* sin for us, who knew no sin; that we might be made the righteousness of God in him.

2 Corinthians 5:21

4. He is the Savior who rose from the grave with full justification for all who believe on His name and His work on their behalf.

Now upon the first *day* of the week, very early in the morning, they came unto the sepulchre, bringing the spices which they had prepared, and certain *others* with them. And they found the stone rolled away from the sepulchre. And they entered in, and found not the body of the Lord Jesus. And it came to pass, as they were much perplexed thereabout, behold, two men stood by them in shining garments: And as they were afraid, and bowed down *their* faces to the earth, they said unto them, Why seek ye the living among the dead? He is not here, but is risen: remember how he spake unto we when he was yet in Galilee, Saying, The Son of man must be delivered into the hands of sinful men, and be crucified, and the third day rise again. And they remembered His Words, And returned from the sepulchre, and told all these things unto the eleven, and to all the rest.

Luke 24:1-9

5. He is the blessed Redeemer who walked among men for a time after his resurrection giving proofs to men of His victory over all sin and death, teaching how His life and perfect cross work fulfilled the holy prophecies of the Christ.

> The former treatise have I made, O Theophilus, of all that Jesus began both to do and teach, Until the day in which he was taken up, after that he through the Holy Ghost had given commandments unto the apostles whom he had chosen: To whom also he shewed himself alive after his passion by many infallible proofs, being seen of them forty days, and speaking of the things pertaining to the kingdom of God.
>
> Acts 1:1-3

> And, behold, two of them went that same day to a village called Emmaus, which was from Jerusalem *about* threescore furlongs. And they talked together of all these things which had happened. And it came to pass, that, while they communed *together* and reasoned, Jesus himself drew near, and went with them. But their eyes were holden that they should not know him.
>
> Then he said unto them, O fools, and slow of heart to believe all that the prophets have spoken: Ought not Christ to have suffered these things, and to enter into his glory? And beginning at Moses and all the prophets, he expounded unto them in all the scriptures the things concerning himself.
>
> And it came to pass, as he sat at meat with them, he took bread, and blessed *it*, and brake, and

gave to them. And their eyes were opened, and they knew him; and he vanished out of their sight. And they said one to another, Did not our heart burn within us, while he talked with us by the way, and while he opened to us the scriptures?

Luke 24:13-16, 25-27, 30-32

Now when *Jesus* was risen early the first *day* of the week, he appeared first to Mary Magdalene, out of whom he had cast seven devils. *And* she went and told them that had been with him, as they mourned and wept. And they, when they had heard that he was alive, and had been seen of her, believed not. After that he appeared in another form unto two of them, as they walked, and went into the country. And they went and told *it* unto the residue: neither believed they them. Afterward he appeared unto the eleven as they sat at meat, and upbraided them with their unbelief and hardness of heart, because they believed not them which had seen him after he was risen.

Mark 16:9-14

Moreover, brethren, I declare unto you the gospel which I preached unto you, which also ye have received, and wherein ye stand; By which also ye are saved, if ye keep in memory what I preached unto you, unless ye have believed in vain. For I delivered unto you first of all that which I also received, how that Christ died for our sins according to the scriptures; And that he was buried, and that he rose again the third day according to the scriptures: And that he was seen of Cephas, then of the twelve: After that, he was seen of above five hundred brethren at once; of whom the greater part remain unto this present, but some are fallen asleep. After that, he was seen of James; then of all the apostles. And last of all he was seen of me also, as of one born out of due time.

1 Corinthians 15:1-8

6. He is the great High Priest who ascended bodily into heaven to sit on the right hand of God where He lives to intercede for all of His saints who are still on earth.

And when he had spoken these things, while they beheld, he was taken up; and a cloud received him out of their sight.

Acts 1:9

When they heard these things, they were cut to the heart, and they gnashed on him with *their* teeth. But he, being full of the Holy Ghost, looked up stedfastly into heaven, and saw the glory of God, and Jesus standing on the right hand of God, And said, Behold, I see the heavens opened, and the Son of man standing on the right hand of God.

Acts 7:54-56

Who *is* he that condemneth? *It is* Christ that died, yea rather, that is risen again, who is even at the right hand of God, who also maketh intercession for us.

Romans 8:34

Seeing then that we have a great high priest, that is passed into the heavens, Jesus the Son of God, let us hold fast *our* profession. For we have not an high priest which cannot be touched with the feeling of our infirmities; but was in all points tempted like as *we are, yet* without sin. Let us therefore come boldly unto the throne of grace, that we may obtain mercy, and find grace to help in time of need.

Hebrews 4:14-16

7. He is the only mediator between God and man.

I am the way, the truth, and the life: no man cometh unto the Father, but by me.

John 14:6

For *there is* one God, and one mediator between God and men, the man Christ Jesus; Who gave himself a ransom for all, to be testified in due time.

1 Timothy 2:5-6

8. He is the possessor of the only name by which man can be saved.

Be it known unto we all, and to all the people of Israel, that by the name of Jesus Christ of Nazareth, whom ye crucified, whom God raised from the dead, *even* by him doth this man stand here before you whole. This is the stone which was set at nought of we builders, which is become the head of the corner. Neither is there salvation in any other: for there is none other name under heaven given among men, whereby we must be saved.

Acts 4:10-12

9. He is the good Shepherd who leads His sheep safely through the hills and valleys of this life.

The LORD *is* my shepherd; I shall not want. He maketh me to lie down in green pastures: he leadeth me beside the still waters. He restoreth my soul: he leadeth me in the paths of righteousness for his name's sake. Yea, though I walk through the valley of the shadow of death, I will fear no evil: for thou *art* with me; thy rod and thy staff they comfort me. Thou preparest a table before me in the presence of mine enemies: thou anointest my head with oil; my cup runneth over. Surely goodness and mercy shall follow me all the days of my life: and I will dwell in the house of the LORD for ever.

Psalm 23

I am the good shepherd: the good shepherd giveth his life for the sheep. But he that is an hireling, and not the shepherd, whose own the sheep are not, seeth the wolf coming, and leaveth the sheep, and fleeth: and the wolf catcheth them, and scattereth the sheep. The hireling fleeth, because he is an hireling, and careth not for the sheep. I am the good shepherd, and know my *sheep*, and am known of mine. As the Father knoweth me, even so know I the Father: and I lay down my life for the sheep. And other sheep I have, which are not of this fold: them also I must bring, and they shall hear my voice; and there shall be one fold, *and* one shepherd. Therefore doth my Father love me, because I lay down my life, that I might take it again. No man taketh it from me, but I lay it down of myself. I have power to lay it down, and I have power to take it again. This commandment have I received of my Father.

John 10:11-18

10. He is the Creator of all things.

Who is the image of the invisible God, the first-born of every creature: For by him were all things created, that are in heaven, and that are in earth, visible and invisible, whether *they be* thrones, or dominions, or principalities, or powers: all things were created by him, and for him: And he is before all things, and by him all things consist.

Colossians 1:15-17

11. He is the sustainer of all things.

God, who at sundry times and in diverse manners spake in time past unto the fathers by the prophets, Hath in these last days spoken unto us by *his* Son, whom he hath appointed heir of all things, by whom also he made the worlds; Who being the brightness of *his* glory, and the express image of his person, and upholding all things by the word of his power, when he had by himself purged our sins, sat down on the right hand of the Majesty on high; Being made so much better than the angels, as he hath by inheritance obtained a more excellent name than they.

Hebrews 1:1-4

12. He is the Lord who rules over heaven and earth.

Wherefore I also, after I heard of your faith in the Lord Jesus, and love unto all the saints, Cease not to give thanks for you, making mention of you in my prayers; That the God of our Lord Jesus Christ, the Father of glory, may give unto you the spirit of wisdom and revelation in the knowledge of him: The eyes of your understanding being enlightened; that ye may know what is the hope of his calling, and what the riches of the glory of his inheritance in the saints, And what *is* the exceeding greatness of his power to us-ward who believe, according to the working of his mighty power, Which he wrought in Christ, when he raised him from the dead, and set *him* at his own right hand in the heavenly *places*, Far above all principality, and power, and might, and dominion, and every name that is named, not only in this world, but also in that which is to come: And hath put all *things* under his feet, and gave him *to be* the head over all *things* to the church, Which is his body, the fulness of him that filleth all in all.

Ephesians 1:15-23

13. He is the Redeemer who will one day return in the clouds to gather all real Christians from the earth before the beginning of the "the wrath to come" (1 Thessalonians 1:10), the final and great Tribulation that is to come on all the earth to try the souls of all men.

> Let not your heart be troubled: ye believe in God, believe also in me. In my Father's house are many mansions: if *it were* not *so*, I would have told you. I go to prepare a place for you. And if I go and prepare a place for you, I will come again, and receive you unto myself; that where I am, *there* ye may be also.
>
> John 14:1-3

> For if we believe that Jesus died and rose again, even so them also which sleep in Jesus will God bring with him. For this we say unto you by the word of the Lord, that we which are alive *and* remain unto the coming of the Lord shall not prevent them which are asleep. For the Lord himself shall descend from heaven with a shout, with the voice of the archangel, and with the trump of God: and the dead in Christ shall rise first: Then we which are alive *and* remain shall be caught up together with them in the clouds, to meet the Lord in the air: and so shall we ever be with the Lord. Wherefore comfort one another with these words.
>
> 1 Thessalonians 4:14-18

> Behold, I shew you a mystery; We shall not all sleep, but we shall all be changed, In a moment, in the twinkling of an eye, at the last trump: for the trumpet

shall sound, and the dead shall be raised incorruptible, and we shall be changed. For this corruptible
must put on incorruption, and this mortal *must* put
on immortality. So when this corruptible shall have
put on incorruption, and this mortal shall have put
on immortality, then shall be brought to pass the saying that is written, Death is swallowed up in victory.

1 Corinthians 15:51-54

For the grace of God that bringeth salvation hath
appeared to all men, Teaching us that, denying
ungodliness and worldly lusts, we should live so-
berly, righteously, and godly, in this present world;
Looking for that blessed hope, and the glorious
appearing of the great God and our Saviour Jesus
Christ; Who gave himself for us, that he might re-
deem us from all iniquity, and purify unto himself
a peculiar people, zealous of good works. These
things speak, and exhort, and rebuke with all authority. Let no man despise thee.

Titus 2:11-15

For God hath not appointed us to wrath, but to obtain salvation by our Lord Jesus Christ, Who died
for us, that, whether we wake or sleep, we should live
together with him. Wherefore comfort yourselves
together, and edify one another, even as also ye do.

1 Thessalonians 5:9-11

14. He is the King of kings who will return bodily to the earth at the end of the Great Tribulation to end the persecution of His earthly people, Israel, and His saints who were saved during that time, and to put an end to the rule of the Gentile nations on the earth and their rebellion against Him and His truth.

For as in Adam all die, even so in Christ shall all be made alive. But every man in his own order: Christ the firstfruits; afterward they that are Christ's at his coming. Then *cometh* the end, when he shall have delivered up the kingdom to God, even the Father; when he shall have put down all rule and all authority and power.

1 Corinthians 15:22-24

And I saw heaven opened, and behold a white horse; and he that sat upon him *was* called Faithful and True, and in righteousness he doth judge and make war. His eyes we*re* as a flame of fire, and on his head we*re* many crowns; and he had a name written, that no man knew, but he himself. And he *was* clothed with a vesture dipped in blood: and his name is called The Word of God. And the armies *which were* in heaven followed him upon white horses, clothed in fine linen, white and clean. And out of his mouth goeth a sharp sword, that with it he should smite the nations: and he shall rule them with a rod of iron: and he treadeth the winepress of the fierceness and wrath of Almighty God. And he hath on *his* vesture and on his thigh a name written, King of kings, and Lord of lords.

Revelation 19:11-16

15. He is the Judge before whom all men shall stand to be judged according to their works.

> For the Father judgeth no man, but hath committed all judgment unto the Son: That all *men* should honour the Son, even as they honour the Father. He that honoureth not the Son honoureth not the Father which hath sent him.
>
> John 5:22
>
> In the day when God shall judge the secrets of men by Jesus Christ according to my gospel.
>
> Romans 2:16

> For we must all appear before the judgment seat of Christ; that every one may receive the things *done* in *his* body, according to that he hath done, whether *it be* good or bad.
>
> 2 Corinthians 5:10

> And I saw a great white throne, and him that sat on it, from whose face the earth and the heaven fled away; and there was found no place for them. And I saw the dead, small and great, stand before God; and the books were opened: and another book was opened, which is *the book* of life: and the dead were judged out of those things which were written in the books, according to their works.
>
> Revelation 20:11-12

16. He is God, who alone can save.

> In the beginning was the Word, and the Word
> was with God, and the Word was God … And the
> Word was made flesh, and dwelt among us, (and
> we beheld his glory, the glory as of the only begot-
> ten of the Father,) full of grace and truth.
>
> John 1:1, 14

> Jesus said unto them, verily, verily, I say unto you,
> before Abraham was, I am.
>
> John 8:58

> Let not your heart be troubled: ye believe in God,
> believe also in me … Jesus saith unto him, I am
> the way, the truth, and the life: no man cometh
> unto the Father, but by me. If ye had known me,
> ye should have known my Father also: and from
> henceforth ye know him, and have seen him … He
> that hath seen me hath seen the Father.
>
> John 14:6-9

> Then came the Jews round about him, and said
> unto him, How long dost thou make us to doubt?
> If thou be the Christ, tell us plainly. Jesus answered
> them, I told you, and ye believed not: the works
> that I do in my Father's name, they bear witness
> of me. But ye believe not, because ye are not of my
> sheep, as I said unto you. My sheep hear my voice,
> and I know them, and they follow me: And I give
> unto them eternal life; and they shall never perish,
> neither shall any *man* pluck them out of my hand.
> My Father, which gave *them* me, is greater than

all; and no *man* is able to pluck *them* out of my Father's hand. I and *my* Father are one.

John 10:24-30

Who being the brightness of *his* [i.e., God's] glory, and the express image [i.e., exact copy] of his person, and upholding all things by the word of his power, when he had by himself purged our sins, sat down on the right hand of the Majesty on high.

Hebrews 1:3

Beware lest any man spoil you through philosophy and vain deceit, after the tradition of men, after the rudiments of the world, and not after Christ. For in him dwelleth all the fullness of the Godhead bodily.

Colossians 2:8-9

One would expect everyone who claims the name of Christ to confess this fundamental of the faith. Yet, as has been pointed out earlier, many such as Mormons, Jehovah's Witnesses, etc. do not. The Word of Faith or Faith Movement is especially blasphemous on this point.

So far we have seen Faith teachers re-create man in the image of God, demote God to the status of man, and deify Satan as a god. Now in concert with the cults and world religions we will see them go so far as to demote Christ to the status of a mere mortal. Creflo Dollar is particularly dogmatic in this regard. Incredibly, he dismisses those who hold that Christ was divine during His earthly sojorn as mere "fantasy preachers":

> And somebody said, well, Jesus came as God! Well, how many of you know the Bible says God never sleeps nor slumbers? And yet in the book of Mark we see Jesus asleep in the back of the boat. Please listen to me. Please listen to me. This ain't no heresy. I'm not some false prophet. I'm just reading this thing out to you of the Bible. I'm just telling you, all these fantasy preachers have been preaching all of this stuff for all these years, and we bought the package.[1]

While Creflo demotes Christ to a mere mortal due to a misunderstanding of the Scriptures, [Ken] Copeland does so on the basis of a personal prophesy from the lips of Messiah Himself. Here's what Christ supposedly told Copeland:

> Don't be disturbed when people put you down and speak harshly and roughly of you. They spoke that way of Me, should they not speak that way of you? The more you get to be like Me, the more they're going to think that way of you. They crucified Me for claiming that I was God. But I didn't claim I was God; I just claimed I walked with Him and that He was in Me. Hallelujah.

When challenged concerning his blasphemy, Copeland retorted, "I didn't say Jesus wasn't God, I said He [*Jesus*] didn't claim to be God when He lived on the earth. Search the Gospels for yourself. If you do, you'll find what I say is true."

If Faith followers would follow the suggestion to search the Gospels, they would discover that they have been horribly misled. [Note the author goes into great detail to show clearly that Christ did, indeed, declare His deity] ... After searching the Gospels, we are left on the horns of a dilemma. Either Jesus forgot that He had testified to His deity during His earthly sojourn, or conversations such as those claimed by Copeland are mere figments of an overactive imagination.[2]

Whosoever transgresseth, and abideth not in the doctrine of Christ, hath not God...
If there come any unto you, and bring not this doctrine, receive him not into *your* house, neither bid him God speed:
For he that biddeth him God speed is partaker of his evil deeds.
2 John 1:9-10

Can I Know for Certain That I'm Saved?

Yes!

Unfortunately, as the unscriptural dogmas of the historic Council of Trent[1] illustrate, vast portions of professing Christendom do not believe this. The following are a very few of the decrees issued by this council that pertain to the subject of this chapter. As you will see, these canons address doctrines or beliefs that Catholic leadership consider "anathema" or damnable heresies. These and their companion canons continue to serve as the foundation for Catholic doctrine today.[2]

The Council of Trent, The Sixth Session: StrongJustification Canons

CANON XV.-If any one saith, that a man, who is born again and justified, is bound of faith to believe that he is assuredly in the number of the predestinate; let him be anathema.

CANON XVI.-If any one saith, that he will for certain, of an absolute and infallible certainty, have that great gift of perseverance unto the end, unless he have learned this by special revelation; let him be anathema.

CANON XXIV.-If any one saith, that the justice received is not preserved and also increased before God through good works; but that the said works are merely the fruits and signs of Justification obtained, but not a cause of the increase thereof; let him be anathema.

CANON XXX.-If any one saith, that, after the grace of Justification has been received, to every penitent sinner the guilt is remitted, and the debt of eternal punishment is blotted out in such wise, that there remains not any debt of temporal punishment to be discharged either in this world, or in the next in Purgatory, before the entrance to the kingdom of heaven can be opened (to him); let him be anathema.

What peace is there in a faith that includes doubt? What security is there in a salvation that rests on the insubstantial sand foundation of man's good works and presumptive ecclesiastical traditions and authority rather than on the rock foundation of the finished cross work of Jesus Christ, which was accomplished according to the eternal and perfect will of God?

By the which will we are sanctified through the offering of the body of Jesus Christ once *for all*. And
every priest standeth daily ministering and offering
oftentimes the same sacrifices, which can never take
away sins: But this man, after he had offered one
sacrifice for sins for ever, sat down on the right hand
of God; From henceforth expecting till his enemies
be made his footstool. For by one offering he hath
perfected for ever them that are sanctified.

Hebrews 10:10-14

The Council of Trent was wrong. Salvation is secured by
grace alone and is eternally secure. And, blessedly, the true
believer can know for certain that this perfect salvation is his.

When the believers in the early church were having
their faith challenged and their confidence in their salvation attacked, the Holy Spirit used the Apostle John
to strengthen them and build up their precious faith. He
concluded his letter of gentle instruction with these words
of encouragement: "These things have I written unto you
that believe on the name of the Son of God; that ye may
know that ye have eternal life" (1 John 5:13).

If one loves someone, he wants God's best for him. If
he is a Christian, he wants him to be saved, and to enjoy
the peace of God's full assurance of his eternal salvation.
While one does not have the right to judge another's eternal salvation, he can, like Peter, exhort those he loves to
"make [their] calling and election sure" (2 Peter 1:10). And
as the Apostle Paul did to the saints at Corinth, he can
lovingly encourage all to "Examine yourselves, whether ye
be in the faith; prove your own selves. Know ye not your

own selves, how that Jesus Christ is in you, except ye be reprobates?" (2 Corinthians 13:5).

God loves His children and wants them to have full assurance that their salvation is both real and eternal, i.e., to have His peace "which passeth all understanding" (Philippians 4:7). So that they might be sure of their salvation, He has provided the following evidences of saving faith as outlined in John's first letter.

If you truly have been born again by the work of God's Holy Spirit, you will:

1. Desire communion, i.e., intimate fellowship, with Christ.[3]

The Lord is more than a "power" or "force" in the true Christian's life. He is truly an intimate friend. Paul tells us that "The Spirit itself beareth witness with our spirit, that we are the children of God" (Romans 8:16). This witness is universal to all who are saved, and results in a response from the new child of God of "Abba, Father" (Romans 8:15), which is a tender expression of confidence indicating both relationship and trust. If you are truly born-again, you will desire and seek the personal fellowship of your Savior.

2. Recognize, abhor, and faithfully confess personal sin.[4]

When you is saved, all your sins are forgiven. But you still have what the Bible calls "the old man, which is corrupt according to the deceitful lusts" (Ephesians 4:22) of the sin nature. Given this, you will sin. You will experience a battle within your soul between the indwelling Holy Spirit and the "old man" and its desire to sin. When you sin, the Spirit will be grieved and condemn you for your disobedience. Upon being convicted of the sin in your life, you will "run" to the Lord in prayer and confess your sin so that your peace and fellowship with your Lord is restored. You will take God's side against yourself. This is a sure sign you are God's child.

3. Delight in and have a deepening commitment to understanding and obeying God's Word.[5]

Men are born again by the Word of God through which He speaks to their heart.[6] If you are a true child of God you will want to hear more and more from your heavenly Father. You will desire to learn more and more about your Friend and Savior, and to understand more about your responsibilities and privileges as a "joint heir with Christ" (Romans 8:17). You will gain all of this knowledge and more from reading, studying, and sharing God's Word. It truly will become spiritual bread, water, and meat to you.

4. Have a sincere compassion and love for fellow believers.[7]

The true church is called the body of Christ.[8] It is composed of all true believers. If you are truly saved, you will have fellowship with both the Lord Jesus Christ and His body. If you truly love the Lord Jesus Christ, you will love other Christians and want to be around them, especially the local gathering of believers in whose fellowship the Lord has placed you.

5.   Have a noticeable change of desires and behavior from worldliness to godliness.[9]

If saved, you have received the life of Christ. Paul expressed this precious truth in this way:

> I am crucified with Christ: nevertheless I live; yet not I, but Christ liveth in me: and the life which I now live in the flesh I live by the faith of the Son of God, who loved me, and gave himself for me.
>
> Galatians 2:20

Peter gives a similar exhortation:

> But as he which hath called you is holy, so be ye holy in all manner of conversation.
>
> 1 Peter 1:15

Worldliness and godliness cannot coexist. One or the other must rule. The real Christian is being continuously molded by the work of the indwelling Spirit "unto a perfect ["complete"] man" (Ephesians 4:13) so that his life increasingly will be "to the praise of his glory, who first trusted in Christ" (Ephesians 1:12).

6.   Show an increasing personal conformity to Christ-likeness[10]

Christians are called "the sons of God," the "children of God," and "joint heirs with Christ." When finally in heaven with the Lord in their glorified bodies, they "shall be like him." In giving instruction to Christian husbands, Paul provides a glimpse of this work of Christ:

> Husbands, love your wives, even as Christ also loved the church, and gave himself for it; That he might sanctify and cleanse it with the washing of water by the word, That he might present it to himself a glorious church, not having spot, or wrinkle, or any such thing; but that it should be holy and without blemish.
>
> Ephesians 5:25-27

That this work will be completed is certain. For the Word tells us that "he which hath begun a good work in you will perform [complete] it until the day of Jesus Christ" (Philippians 1:6). This process of becoming like the Lord begins as soon as you are saved and progresses throughout your life on earth.

7. Experience undeserved conflict with the world.[11]

The Lord warns believers that:

> If the world hates you, ye know that it hated me before *it hated* you. If ye were of the world, the world would love his own: but because ye are not of the world, but I have chosen you out of the world, therefore the world hateth you. Remember

the word that I said unto you, The servant is not greater than his lord. If they have persecuted me, they will also persecute you; if they have kept my saying, they will keep yours also.

John 15:18-20

James tells his readers very bluntly,

Know ye not that the friendship of the world is enmity [hatred] with God? Whosoever therefore will be a friend of the world is the enemy of God.

James 4:4

If you are truly a Christian you are instructed "as much as lieth in" you to "be at peace with all men" (Romans 12:18). However, you are not to love "the world, neither the things that are in the world" (1 John 2:15). Because you are saved and not "of" the world anymore, the world will not always deal with you in the loving manner in which you are exhorted by God's Word to deal with them. God's Spirit in you will make you different, and that difference will manifest itself. You will be separated from the world to a significant degree.

8. Have increasing confidence in and fellowship with the Lord in prayer.[12]

As has already been noted, one of the first acts of a new Christian is to cry "Abba, Father" (Romans 8:15). This first prayer of a newly born child of God is the most tender of expressions and initiates an increasingly intimate relationship with the believer's God and Lord. It is the clear witness to the new Father-child relationship that has been formed by faith.

The Word also explains that Christ and His church share another relationship: that of Bridegroom and bride. If you are a real Christian, as you travel through life and grow in faith, your familiarity with your Lord and your pleasure in His company will increase, and you will increasingly seek His presence, affection, and direction for your life. And just as an earthly bride grows closer to and wants to be with and communicate with her fiancé more as her wedding day approaches, so it will be with you. You will seek His face in prayer more often and more effectively with each passing day of your life in Him, desiring His promised return with increasing fervor.

A twentieth-century saint once gave a "short list" of the evidences of personal salvation, which serves as a simple but provocative complement to what has been shared above.

> If I see, with a feeling sense in my heart, what a heinous and filthy thing all sin is, what a depraved and loathsome creature I am by nature, what a sink of iniquity still remains within me, what a suitable and sufficient Savior Christ is for such a wretch as me, what a lovely and desirable thing holiness is, then I must have been called to life. If I am now conscious of holy desires and endeavors to which I was previously a stranger, then I must be alive in Christ.[13]

Though unconfessed and unforsaken sin will hinder the maturation or expression of the evidences of saving faith outlined above, all real Christians will manifest all of these to some degree. And these fruits will become more pronounced as the Christian walks with the Lord in love and obedience.

If these brief reflections do not assure your heart or if something still seems to be missing, there may be at least two reasons for the uneasiness:

1. Though saved, you may not be walking "in the Spirit" (Galatians 5:16). In other words, you may be walking according to your own will. If you are, though you are a Christian, you are out of fellowship with your Lord so that you are not enjoying the peace of God for "God is not mocked" (Galatians 6:7). In this case, you have these gracious assurances to encourage you to deal honestly with your sins:

   > My little children, these things write I unto you, that ye sin not. And if any man sin, we have an advocate with the Father, Jesus Christ the righteous:
   > 1 John 2:1

   > If we confess our sins, he is faithful and just to forgive us *our* sins, and to cleanse us from all unrighteousness.
   > 1 John 1:9

2. Or your uneasiness may be because you are not truly saved! This may be difficult to admit, but your eternal destiny depends on the reality of your salvation, not an

intellectual hope. You must be honest with yourself. You must be sure.

Herein is love, not that we loved God, but that he loved us, and sent his Son to be the propitiation for our sins.

1 John 4:10

God commendeth his love toward us, in that, while we were yet sinners, Christ died for us.

Romans 5:8

There is therefore now no condemnation to them which are in Christ Jesus, who walk not after the flesh, but after the Spirit. For the law of the Spirit of life in Christ Jesus hath made me free from the law of sin and death. For what the law could not do, in that it was weak through the flesh, God sending his own Son in the likeness of sinful flesh, and for sin, condemned sin in the flesh: That the righteousness of the law might be fulfilled in us, who walk not after the flesh, but after the Spirit. For they that are after the flesh do mind the things of the flesh; but they that are after the Spirit the things of the Spirit. For to be carnally minded *is* death; but to be spiritually minded *is* life and peace. Because the carnal mind *is* enmity against God: for it is not subject to the law of God, neither indeed can be. So then they that are in the flesh cannot please God. But ye are not in the flesh, but in the Spirit, if so be that the Spirit of God dwell in you. Now if any man have not the Spirit of Christ, he is none of his.

Romans 8:1-9

The word is nigh thee, even in thy mouth, and in thy heart: that is, the word of faith, which we have preached; That if thou shalt confess with thy mouth the Lord Jesus, and shalt believe in thine heart that God hath raised him from the dead, thou shalt be saved...For whosoever shall call upon the name of the Lord shall be saved.

Romans 10:9, 13

Recommended reading:

Absolutely Sure, Steve Lawson, Multnomah Publishers, Sisters, Oregon

God Is Not Like Man, but True Believers Are to Be Like God!

Man is without excuse. God warns about the sin of redefining His glorious holiness into an image formed according to man's vain imagination and carnal, humanistic standards. He warns against assuming that He, the Creator, is like man, the creature:

> But unto the wicked God saith, What hast thou to do to declare my statutes, or *that* thou shouldest take my covenant in thy mouth? Seeing thou hatest instruction, and castest my words behind thee. When thou sawest a thief, then thou consentedst with him, and hast been partaker with adulterers. Thou givest thy mouth to evil, and thy tongue frameth deceit. Thou sittest *and* speakest against thy brother; thou slanderest thine own mother's son. These *things* hast thou done, and I kept silence; thou thoughtest that I was altogether *such an one* as thyself: *but* I will re-

prove thee, and set *them* in order before thine eyes.
Now consider this, ye that forget God, lest I tear *you*
in pieces, and *there be* none to deliver.

Psalm 50:16-22

As His Word makes clear, God will judge sin. He is not,
nor will He ever be, mocked by man's self-righteousness.
"Be not deceived; God is not mocked: for whatsoever a
man soweth, that shall he also reap" (Galatians 6:7).

Yet, while God is not like man, His Word teaches us
that true believers are to be like Him, reflecting His glory
in their lives! Listen to A.W. Tozer as he speaks to both
sides of the doctrinal coin of God's holiness.

> God is holy with an absolute holiness that knows
> no degrees, and this He cannot impart to His crea-
> tures. But there is a relative and contingent holi-
> ness which He shares with angels and seraphim in
> heaven and with redeemed men on earth as their
> preparation for heaven. This holiness God can and
> does impart to His children … No honest man can
> say "I am holy," but neither is any honest man
> willing to ignore the solemn words of the inspired
> writer, "Follow peace with all men, and holiness,
> without which no man shall see the Lord."
>
> Caught in this dilemma, what are we Christians
> to do? We must hide our unholiness in the wounds
> of Christ as Moses hid himself in the cleft of the
> rock while the glory of God passed by … we must
> believe that God sees us perfect in His Son while
> He disciplines and chastens and purges us that we
> may be partakers of His holiness.[1]

God's grace is not a license to sin. It is the means by which the true believer is freed *from* sin. It is the manifestation of the transforming love of God that provokes the believer to honor and glorify His God and Savior.

> For the love of Christ constraineth us; because we thus judge, that if one died for all, then were all dead: And *that* he died for all, that they which live should not henceforth live unto themselves, but unto him which died for them, and rose again.
>
> 2 Corinthians 5:14-15

God's grace saves from the bondage of sin. Before salvation, man is enslaved by his sin nature, a creature of sin and a vessel of sinfulness. However, when one is saved, he is freed from the rule of sin over his life by the power of the blood of Christ. Receiving the life of Christ, he is endowed with the power to overcome sin and, thereby, live for the glory of God. He does this by willingly and joyfully living a godly life for the sake of God's honor by the strength and wisdom provided by His indwelling Spirit.

Paul wrote the following words to encourage saints of all ages:

> For the grace of God that bringeth salvation hath appeared to all men, Teaching us that, denying ungodliness and worldly lusts, we should live soberly, righteously, and godly, in this present world; Looking for that blessed hope, and the glorious appearing of the great God and our Saviour Jesus Christ; Who gave himself for us, that he might re-

deem us from all iniquity, and purify unto himself
a peculiar people, zealous of good works. These
things speak, and exhort, and rebuke with all authority. Let no man despise thee.

Titus 2:11-15

Having therefore these promises, dearly beloved, let
us cleanse ourselves from all filthiness of the flesh
and spirit, perfecting holiness in the fear of God.

2 Corinthians 7:1

In his letter to the Colossians, Paul further expounds on
this twofold work of true, saving faith as follows:

If ye then be risen with Christ, seek those things
which are above, where Christ sitteth on the right
hand of God. Set your affection on things above,
not on things on the earth. For ye are dead, and
your life is hid with Christ in God. When Christ,
who is our life, shall appear, then shall ye also appear with him in glory. Mortify therefore your
members which are upon the earth; fornication,
uncleanness, inordinate affection, evil concupis-
cence, and covetousness, which is idolatry: For
which things' sake the wrath of God cometh on
the children of disobedience: In the which ye also
walked some time, when ye lived in them. But now
ye also put off all these; anger, wrath, malice, blasphemy, filthy communication out of your mouth.

Colossians 3:1-8

(A reading of the entire third chapter of Paul's letter to the Colossians will provide a fuller perspective on what is required to truly live for Christ.)

The whole Word of God teaches that there must be a "putting on" in the believer's life of the things of God, which is to say, a putting on of Christ. It is through this inevitable result of saving grace that the life of Christ is manifested in him. In other words, the fruit of the Spirit becomes the fruit of his life and witnesses to those around him that he has truly "risen with Christ." There must also be a corresponding "putting off" of the things of the flesh; i.e., the "old man," the works of his sin nature if God is to be pleased. As Paul said to the Galatians, believers are to "walk in the Spirit" so that they will "*not* fulfill the lusts of the flesh" (Galatians 5:16, italics added).

It is essential to understand this greatest of truths: the Christian's life is a purchased life. Being purchased with the precious blood of the crucified Christ, he owes absolute allegiance to his Owner.[2] A gospel that fails to give a plain presentation of the fact that grace does not free the sinner to live as he wills but rather, to live as God wills, neither glorifies God nor blesses its disciples. The life received through God's grace by faith alone in Jesus Christ alone is to be lived in such a way that God is glorified in all things. Salvation is not about man getting what he wants; it is about giving God what He alone deserves. The believer is not saved to fulfill his own purposes but God's. A gospel that does not clearly teach this mutual sacrifice, i.e., Christ for the saint and the saint for Christ,[3] is "another gospel" that is to be condemned.[4]

> [Christ] gave himself for us, that he might redeem us from all iniquity, and purify unto himself a peculiar people, zealous of good works.
>
> Titus 2:14

> For [God] hath made him *to be* sin for us, who knew no sin; that we might be made the righteousness of God in him.
>
> 2 Corinthians 5:21

In his summary comments regarding the teachings of 2 Corinthians 4, Albert Barnes said this about the kind of life that true, saving faith effects:

> There is no true knowledge of God except that which shines in the face of Jesus Christ (2 Corinthians 4:6). He came to make known the true God. He is the exact image of God. He resembles him in all things. And he who does not love the character of Jesus Christ, therefore, does not love the character of God. He who does not seek to be like Jesus Christ, does not desire to be like God. He who does not bear the image of the Redeemer, does not bear the image of God. To be a moral man merely, therefore, is not to be like God. To be amiable and honest, merely, is not to be like God. Jesus Christ, the image of God, was more than this. He was religious. He was holy. He was, as a man, a man of prayer, and filled with

the love of God, and was always submissive to his holy will. He sought his honour and glory; and he made it the great purpose of his life and death to make known his existence, perfections, and name. To imitate him in this, is to have the knowledge of the glory of God; and no man is like God who does not bear the image of the Redeemer. No man is like God, therefore, who is not a Christian. Of course, no man can be prepared for heaven who is not a friend and follower of Jesus Christ.[5]

A gospel that does not issue a clarion call for selfless obedience to God's will, a walk that reflects His ways, and, in that, the rejection of all self-advancement in favor of His glory is a gospel that is based on wrong facts, utilizes wrong appeals, leads to wrong conclusions, and produces carnal, sinful lives. Such a gospel cannot save. Rather, it leaves its disciples in their sins to ultimately stand before God on Judgment Day confused and without hope, in other words, religious but lost.

The Challenges for Real Christians

In this final chapter, I want to get personal.

That there will be people in hell who now sincerely believe they are Christians is beyond doubt. The real issue before you today is "What can I do about it?"

If you are a real Christian, you should prayerfully reconsider the fate of any loved ones or friends who are involved in organizations or churches that do not preach the biblical Jesus or that compromise the eternal, never-changing faith once delivered to the saints. If they continue in their present faith, it is possible that they will be among those described by our Lord in Matthew 7:21-23, those who sincerely believe they are saved when, in fact, they are headed to eternal damnation. So what should be your attitude toward them? Should it be one of humanistic acceptance and ecumenical love that may produce some kind of superficial, man-centered unity yet leave them substantially unchanged? Only if you want to "love" them right into hell!

We have been saved to be faithful ambassadors for

Christ. Our calling in the Lord combined with our love and compassion for the lost should compel us to take immediate, positive, Bible-based evangelical action, which is characterized in God's Word as "speaking the truth in love" (Ephesians 4:15). We should be sharing with our friends and any others the Lord brings into our life the real truth that saves "to the uttermost [them] that come unto God by him."[1] But such a ministry, though wonderfully rewarding, is challenging.

> And he said to *them* all, If any *man* will come after me, let him deny himself, and take up his cross daily, and follow me. For whosoever will save his life shall lose it: but whosoever will lose his life for my sake, the same shall save it. For what is a man advantaged, if he gain the whole world, and lose himself, or be cast away? For whosoever shall be ashamed of me and of my words, of him shall the Son of man be ashamed, when he shall come in his own glory, and *in his* Father's, and of the holy angels.
>
> Luke 9:23-26

> And now, little children, abide in him; that, when he shall appear, we may have confidence, and not be ashamed before him at his coming.
>
> 1 John 2:28

Rightly Dividing and Defending the Word of God

To be an effective witness for Christ in this age of the great falling away[2] when so many have been deceived into believing they are born-again Christians, you must have a clear understanding of what truly is saving faith. This understanding will come as you willingly submit to the Lord's very plain instructions as given through the Apostle Paul:

> Study to shew thyself approved unto God, a workman that needeth not to be ashamed, rightly dividing the word of truth. But shun profane *and* vain babblings: for they will increase unto more ungodliness.
>
> 2 Timothy 2:15-16

Only when you have prayerfully determined in your own heart to diligently study, understand, and obey God's Word with the Holy Spirit's guidance[3] are you prepared to be faithful to the Lord's exhortation given through the Apostle Peter:

> But sanctify the Lord God in your hearts: and *be* ready always to *give* an answer to every man that asketh you a reason of the hope that is in you with meekness and fear: Having a good conscience; that, whereas they speak evil of you, as of evildoers, they may be ashamed that falsely accuse your good conversation in Christ. For *it is* better, if the will of God be so, that ye suffer for well doing, than for evil doing.
>
> 1 Peter 3:15-17

If your testimony is to be used by the Lord to lead men to the salvation freely offered in Jesus Christ, the "reason" you give for your hope must be the truth, the whole truth, and most importantly, *nothing but the truth*. Vain, man-centered philosophies or psychology cannot save. That is why Paul in his last recorded words gave the young minister Timothy the following charge:

> I charge *thee* therefore before God, and the Lord Jesus Christ, who shall judge the quick and the dead at his appearing and his kingdom; Preach the word; be instant in season, out of season; reprove, rebuke, exhort with all longsuffering and doctrine. For the time will come when they will not endure sound doctrine; but after their own lusts shall they heap to themselves teachers, having itching ears; And they shall turn away *their* ears from the truth, and shall be turned unto fables. But watch thou in all things, endure afflictions, do the work of an evangelist, make full proof of thy ministry.
>
> 2 Timothy 4:1-5

It is the preaching of the sound doctrine of the incorruptible Word of God that saves.[4] God's Word is all that is needed both to bring the message of salvation to lost humanity, and to provide godly counsel to sincere Christians who desire to live God-honoring and blessed lives in the Lord.

> According as his divine power hath given unto us all things that *pertain* unto life and godliness, through the knowledge of him that hath called us to glory and virtue: Whereby are given unto us exceeding great and precious promises: that by these ye might

be partakers of the divine nature, having escaped the corruption that is in the world through lust.

2 Peter 1:3-4

Walking the Talk

But the challenge in these times is not "simply" to have the words of a faithful testimony on our lips. The real challenge is to maintain a walk that faithfully witnesses that the testimony of our lips is sincere.

> Thou therefore endure hardness, as a good soldier of Jesus Christ. No man that warreth entangleth himself with the affairs of *this* life; that he may please him who hath chosen him to be a soldier. And if a man also strives for masteries, *yet* is he not crowned, except he strive lawfully. The husband-man that laboureth must be first partaker of the fruits. Consider what I say; and the Lord give thee understanding in all things.
>
> 2 Timothy 2:3-7

As this passage makes clear, you are called to be a faithful soldier, separated to the work of the Captain of your salvation.[5] Being motivated by love and always charitable in spirit, you must be faithful to the Word of God. And you must understand that the separation to which you are exhorted is two-fold: (1) separation from the world and its temptations, and (2) separation from false doctrines and those who espouse them.

Love not the world, neither the things *that are* in the world. If any man love the world, the love of the Father is not in him. For all that *is* in the world, the lust of the flesh, and the lust of the eyes, and the pride of life, is not of the Father, but is of the world. And the world passeth away, and the lust thereof: but he that doeth the will of God abideth for ever.

1 John 2:15-17

Look to yourselves, that we lose not those things which we have wrought, but that we receive a full reward. Whosoever transgresseth, and abideth not in the doctrine of Christ, hath not God. He that abideth in the doctrine of Christ, he hath both the Father and the Son. If there come any unto you, and bring not this doctrine, receive him not into *your* house, neither bid him God speed: For he that biddeth him God speed is partaker of his evil deeds.

2 John 1:8-11

Failure to heed these plain commands will undermine both the credibility and the ultimate effectiveness of your witness.

Avoiding the Snare of "The End Justifies the Means"

Instead of remaining steadfast in the faith, the vast majority of the professing church of today has rebelled against these plain commands of God by attempting to take His truth to the world by the means of two erroneous growth strategies: (1) assimilation, becoming more like the world so as to make Christianity more acceptable to the worldly, and (2) infiltration, becoming a part of error-filled works in an attempt to influence them from within, a sort of "Trojan Horse" strategy. Both strategies are blatant compromises of Romans 12:1-2:

> I beseech you therefore, brethren, by the mercies of God, that ye present your bodies a living sacrifice, holy, acceptable unto God, *which is* your reasonable service. And be not conformed to this world: but be ye transformed by the renewing of your mind, that ye may prove what *is* that good, and acceptable, and perfect, will of God.

The world has never been won by Christians becoming a part of it. Rather, sinners are saved by the preaching of the pure gospel of grace by a holy church that is separate from and unlike the world. And the message is not "Add Christ to your life and follow us," but "Repent of your sins, die to your own self interests, turn from the world, and pick up your cross daily and follow the Lord." So far as God is concerned, nothing has changed. This is still the way He works.

By bringing worldly practices into its worship on the one hand and attempting to become a part of heretical and even non-Christian organizations in order to influence them from within on the other, the church has become just like the world it is attempting to evangelize: willing to compromise and driven by the erroneous doctrine of "the end justifies the means." As a result of not maintaining its pilgrim character and remaining separate from the world in its practices and doctrines, it has become more superficially attractive to a growing audience (good marketing), but has compromised the truth and dishonored God (sin).

The Day of Judgment is fast approaching. On that day all will answer for their choices. The Judge will not be those in the world that were impressed with this compromised approach to promoting man-defined and man-centered Christianity, but Christ Himself.[6] And the standard by which all will be judged will not be man's opinions but the unchanging, eternal Word of God.

Is your love for the Savior and the lost sufficient to accept the challenge of "speaking the truth in love?"[7] A.W. Tozer brought perspective to difference between the true gospel and the modern man-centered gospel when he compared the "old" cross and the "new."[8]

> The old cross is a symbol of death. It stands for the abrupt, violent end of a human being. The man in Roman times who took up his cross and started down the road had already said good-by to his friends. He was not coming back. He was going out to have it ended. The cross made no compromise, modified nothing, spared nothing; it slew all of the man, completely and for good. It did not try to keep on good terms with its victim. It struck cruel and hard, and when it had finished its work, the man was no more.
>
> The race of Adam is under death sentence. There is no commutation and no escape. God cannot approve any of the fruits of sin, however innocent they may appear or beautiful to the eyes of men. God salvages the individual by liquidating him and then raising him again to newness of life.

That evangelism which draws friendly parallels between the ways of God and the ways of men is false to the Bible and cruel to the souls of its hearers. The faith of Christ does not parallel the world, it intersects it. In coming to Christ we do not bring our old life up onto a higher plane; we leave it at the cross. The corn of wheat must fall into the ground and die.

We who preach the gospel must not think of ourselves as public relations agents sent to establish good will between Christ and the world. We must not imagine ourselves commissioned to make Christ acceptable to big business, the press, the world of sports or modern education. We are not diplomats but prophets, and our message is not a compromise but an ultimatum.

Perhaps the Greatest Challenge of All

At this point you may be saying "You mean there's more!" Well, perhaps what is about to be shared is not so much "more" as a summation of everything that has been said thus far. The "greatest challenge of all" is revealed in the parable of the wheat and the tares.

Another parable put he forth unto them, saying, The kingdom of heaven is likened unto a man which sowed good seed in his field: But while men slept, his enemy came and sowed tares among the wheat, and went his way. But when the blade was sprung up, and brought forth fruit, then appeared the tares also. So the servants of the householder came and said unto him, Sir, didst not thou sow good seed in thy field? from whence then hath it tares? He said unto them, An enemy hath done this. The servants said unto him, Wilt thou then that we go and gather them up? But he said, *Nay; lest while ye gather up the tares, ye root up also the wheat with them.* Let both grow together until the harvest: and in the time of harvest I will say to the reapers, Gather ye together first the tares, and bind them in bundles to burn them: but gather the wheat into my barn.

Matthew 13:24-30

The challenge is suggested by the portion italicized above. No human can truly judge the salvation of another. But the angels can, as evidenced by this parable. However, though it is easy for the heavenly hosts to identify the false from the real, separating them is another matter. Why? Because the lives of the wheat (believers) and the tares (unbelievers) are so intertwined, so interdependent, that to uproot the tares would also uproot the wheat, thereby destroying its ability to produce fruit!

What does this "uprooting" of the wheat mean? Obviously, it does not mean that the wheat, i.e., the true believers, would lose their salvation. Salvation is eternal, the gift of God[9] that can never be lost.

For I came down from heaven, not to do mine own will, but the will of him that sent me. And this is the Father's will which hath sent me, that of all which he hath given me I should lose nothing, but should raise it up again at the last day.

John 6:38-39

What this means is that even true believers are going to be so compromised by the man-centered teachings and influences of the last days that the steadfastness of their own faith will be undermined by the natural relationships they form with the unbelievers around them. Be they family or friends, personal relationships can often undermine real faithfulness. Peace with men can become more important than honoring God. The Lord was very specific in His teaching of this danger, and His personal walk emphasized the priority of relationships in His own life.

> Think not that I am come to send peace on earth: I came not to send peace, but a sword. For I am come to set a man at variance against his father, and the daughter against her mother, and the daughter-in-law against her mother-in-law. And a man's foes *shall be* they of his own household. He that loveth father or mother more than me is not worthy of me: and he that loveth son or daughter more than me is not worthy of me.
>
> Matthew 10:34-37

> While he yet talked to the people, behold, *his* mother and his brethren stood without, desiring to speak with him. Then one said unto him, Behold, thy mother and thy brethren stand without, desiring to speak with thee. But he answered and said unto him that told him, Who is my mother? and who are my brethren? And he stretched forth his hand toward his disciples, and said, Behold my mother and my brethren! For whosoever shall do

the will of my Father which is in heaven, the same
is my brother, and sister, and mother.

Matthew 12:46-50

It is sad to think that blood-washed saints can be so
earthly-minded that they value natural, temporal friendships and relationships and their own comfort and desires
more than the glory of God and the honor and integrity
of His eternal church. But many, if not most, do. The great
Apostle Paul said at the end of his life, "All which are in
Asia be turned away from me ... Demas hath forsaken me,
having loved this present world" (2 Timothy 1:15; 4:10).
Human relationships can be both wonderful and dangerous. Unless governed by true submission to God's eternal
Word and sensitive to the holy influence of His Spirit,
they can actually become competitors to the true faith and
enemies of the true gospel.

So what is the greatest challenge to effective witnessing today (if not in every age): human sentiment that is
in conflict with the commandments of the Word of God.
All the errors of secular humanism are rooted in this. If
you do not remain watchful for this in your own life and
keep it in holy perspective, it will undermine your love of
God and compromise your faithfulness to the proclamation and defense of His Word.

How can you meet this challenge? You can have victory in the Lord by making God's priorities your own by
sincerely and carefully examining all aspects of your life in
the light of the holy Word of God and obeying its truth.

And thou shalt love the Lord thy God with all thy
heart, and with all thy soul, and with all thy mind,
and with all thy strength: this *is* the first commandment. And the second *is* like, *namely* this,
Thou shalt love thy neighbour as thyself. There is
none other commandment greater than these.

Mark12:30-31

Jesus answered and said unto him, if a man love
me, he will keep my words: and my Father will
love him, and we will come unto him, and make
our abode with him. He that loveth me not keep-
eth not my sayings: and the word which ye hear is
not mine, but the Father's which sent me.

John 14:23-24

For this is the love of God, that we keep his commandments: and his commandments are not
grievous.

1 John 5:3

Do you love God more than man, any man? If not, you
will never be an effective witness, will never be fully fruitful in the Lord, and will never enjoy His enduring and
fullest blessings. In fact, you will never be a disciple who
is used to His glory because you will inevitably deal with
partiality toward those you love (family, friends), and
rationalize rather than condemn sin.[10]

Them that sin rebuke before all, that others also
may fear. I charge *thee* before God, and the Lord
Jesus Christ, and the elect angels, that thou ob-

serve these things without preferring one before another, doing nothing by partiality.

1 Timothy 5:20-21

There are few things on earth more wonderful than a natural family that is blessed of the Lord. However, too many Christians are blinded by humanistic love and fail to heed the Lord's own very specific teachings regarding natural relationships, especially our closest kin. As He showed us by His own example, these, like all things in our life, must be placed in subjection to personal faithfulness to the eternal truth and purpose of God. He must be our "all in all" (Ephesians 1:23).

The compromise of God's Word for anyone, even our most precious loved ones, will only bring loss, regardless of the assumed purity of one's motive or goal. The only way to true and enduring blessing is obedience to "all the counsel of God" (Acts 20:27) without personal prejudice or partiality of any kind. To those who live accordingly, the Lord promises rich blessings despite the temporal cost that sometimes may be required.

And when he had called the people *unto him* with his disciples also, he said unto them, Whosoever will come after me, let him deny himself, and take up his cross, and follow me. For whosoever will save his life shall lose it; but whosoever shall lose his life for my sake and the gospel's, the same shall save it.

Mark 8:34-35

And every one that hath forsaken houses, or
brethren, or sisters, or father, or mother, or wife, or
children, or lands, for my name's sake, shall receive
an hundredfold, and shall inherit everlasting life.

Matthew 19:29

A Final Appeal

The following is an excerpt from a commentary given by
Albert Barnes in his overview of 2 Corinthians 4. Though
primarily having the formal ministry in mind, the appli-
cability to every true Christian is inescapable. All of us
are exhorted to carefully examine our personal faith[11] so
that we might "*be* ready always to give an answer to every
man that asketh us a reason of the hope that is in us with
meekness and fear" (1 Peter 3:15).

> In order to animate us in the work to which God
> has called us; to encourage us in our trials; and to
> prompt us to a faithful discharge of our duties, es-
> pecially those who like Paul are called to preach
> the gospel, we should have, like him, the following
> views and feelings—views and feelings adapted to
> sustain us in all our trials, and to uphold us in all
> the conflicts of life:
>
> First: A firm and unwavering belief of the truth
> of the religion which we profess, and of the truth
> which we make known to others, 2 Corinthians
> 4:12 ... He that believes that men are in fact in
> danger of hell, *will* tell them of it; he that be-
> lieves there is an awful bar of judgment, will tell
> them of it; he that believes that the Son of God

became incarnate and died for men, will tell them of it; he that believes that there is a heaven, will invite them to it. And one reason why professing Christians are so reluctant to speak of these things is, that they have no very settled and definite conviction of their truth, and no correct view of their relative importance.

Second: We should have a firm assurance that God has raised up the Lord Jesus, and that we also shall be raised from the dead, 2 Corinthians 4:14. The hope and expectation of the resurrection of the dead was one of the sustaining principles which upheld Paul in his labours ... And so we, if we are assured of this great truth, shall welcome trial also, and shall be able to endure afflictions and persecutions. They will soon be ended; and the eternal glory in the morning of the resurrection shall be more than a compensation for all that we shall endure in this life.

Third: We should have a sincere desire to promote the glory of God, and to bring as many as possible to join in his praise, and to celebrate his saving mercy, 2 Corinthians 4:15 ... No object is so noble as that of endeavoring to promote the Divine glory; and he who is influenced by that, will care little how many sufferings he is called to endure in this life.

Christians should have such a belief of the truth of their religion as to be willing to speak of it at all times, and in all places, 2 Corinthians 4:13. If we have such a belief we shall be willing to speak of it. We cannot help it. We shall so see its value, and so love it, and our hearts will be so full of it, and we shall see so much the danger of our fellow men, that we shall be instinctively prompted to go to them and warn them of their danger, and tell them of the glories of the Redeemer.[12]

We are to live in the glorious expectation that Jesus Christ may return at any moment. Things today are just as He told us they would be in the time of His return. Evil men are growing in both number and influence,[13] the "love of many" is growing cold,[14] and self-willed Christians, let alone mere professors of the Christian faith, are becoming increasingly uninterested in the sound, life-giving, and life-blessing doctrines of the Word of God. Rather, they are seeking out teachers who will "speak unto ... [them] smooth things; prophesy deceits" (Isaiah 30:10) and willingly, though perhaps unknowingly, turning from righteousness to sinful error, from real truth to "fables" (2 Timothy 4:3-4). As a result, there are multitudes today who profess faith in Christ, willingly take His name, are very religious in their faith, but are not saved. They simply do not know Christ, nor He them.[15]

Because of this, the greatest mission field for you today is right where you live, in the professing church and religious world where you walk every day. Our omniscient Lord foresaw this and through His eternal Word exhorts us to be watchful servants who are always "speaking the truth in love" (Ephesians 4:15) as we declare the only Way of salvation.[16] By this means, we glorify our heavenly Father by guarding his Word and the honor of His name in this time of the great falling away.[17]

Does what has been shared with you in this book concern you as much as it does me? It breaks my heart that many sincere individuals who believe they are Christians are unknowingly headed for hell. The need for faithful witnesses for the truth has never been greater. But witnessing to those who already claim the name of Christ, who are self-confident in their professed faith, and who are encouraged in their error by the multitudes around them who are in the same state of confusion is not easy. Fortunately, we have the two things necessary to be successful in our ambassadorship for the Lord: the love of Christ[18] and "the sword of the Spirit, which is the word of God" (Ephesians 6:17).

When I was a young man, I met a girl who was naturally moral, well respected by all who knew her, and considered herself a good Christian, fully assured of heaven. As we got to know one another, I was provoked to give witness for the Lord. But rather than trying to convince her that my faith was the "right" faith through force of argument, I determined to allow the Word of God to convince her of the truth, to let it speak for itself.

I began my witness one day with a simple question that is appropriate to ask anyone who claims to be a Christian: "How were you saved?" Anyone who is truly saved will be anxious to share his experience. But those who are mere professors of the Christian faith will be forced to face the truth that they do not truly understand what *saved* means which will provide an opportunity to open the Word of God with them.

In this case, her answer was basically "I was baptized as an infant and have done 'pretty much' all that I have been instructed to do by the church" with an added "I think

I'm a good person." This allowed me to show her from the Word that neither water baptism nor good works can save a person, which prepared the way to lay down the one foundation[19] upon which all faithful witness rests: salvation by grace alone through faith alone in Jesus Christ alone. Thereafter, each time we would meet, I would share a little more of my personal testimony and gently provoke her to express her own beliefs and explain why she believed as she did. I would then take her to that part of the Word of God that either supported or contradicted each belief. As we progressed in our friendly study of God's Word, two things happened. First, she came to see for herself that the faith she had been taught was not the faith the Bible taught. She saw her need for salvation as her eyes were opened by the Spirit to see the true faith of Jesus Christ, and she received Jesus as her personal Lord and Savior. Second, we fell in love, and she became my faithful and ever-patient wife, the amazingly talented mother of our fabulous three children, and the wonderful grandmother of our eleven (as of this writing) marvelous grandchildren.

While being faithful to God's Word may not bring you a spouse, at least not in the same manner it did me, it will make you an effective witness and fruitful servant to God's glory. Don't be ashamed of the gospel. Trust God and His Word. His truth saves. When rightly divided and shared at His direction without compromise, it will never fail to accomplish His will.

> So shall my word be that goeth forth out of my mouth: it shall not return unto me void, but it shall

accomplish that which I please, and it shall prosper *in the thing* whereto I sent it.

Isaiah 55:11

I hope this small work will provoke you to enlist as a fellow warrior in the intensifying spiritual battle for the everlasting truth, to be a faithful laborer in the Lord's great harvest. May God's Spirit encourage and empower you to that end.

> And many of them that sleep in the dust of the earth shall awake, some to everlasting life, and some to shame *and* everlasting contempt. And they that be wise shall shine as the brightness of the firmament; and they that turn many to righteousness as the stars for ever and ever.

Daniel 12:1-2

> They that sow in tears shall reap in joy. He that goeth forth and weepeth, bearing precious seed, shall doubtless come again with rejoicing, bringing his sheaves *with him.*

Psalm 126:5–6

Die to yourself and love the Lord with your whole heart. Only then will you truly have compassion for the lost. Only then will you serve God acceptably. The challenge lies within. The victory comes from forsaking all the idols of this life, and willingly and lovingly submitting everything in your life to God. When His glory is your only motive and goal, you will be fruitful in your service to Him and a true blessing to all you love.

Endnotes

Christians in Hell?

1. Matthew 5:21-22, 27-28; 12:36-37; Luke 12:2-3; Hebrews 4:12-13

2. *The Training of the Twelve*, A.B. Bruce, Kregel Publications, Grand Rapids, MI, pg 109

Hearing Only or Hearing and Doing?

1. *Romans, Exposition of chapters 3:20-4:25—Atonement and Justification*, D. Martyn Lloyd-Jones, The Banner of Truth Trust, pg 19

2. James 1:22

3. Taken from the Sunday, October 22, 2006 article, "Prince of darkness," Steve Arney, Pantagraph newspaper, Bloomington, IL

4. A.W. Tozer quote, http://thinkexist.com/quotation/one_hundred_religious_persons_knit_into_a_unity/264646.html

The Power and Deceit of Man-Centered Religion

1. 2 Peter 2:3

2. Foundation Magazine, www.feasite.org

3. *I Have Seen The Lord*, Easter Sunday, April 12, 2009, John Piper, www.desiringgod.org/ResourceLibrary/Sermons/ByDate/2009/3812_I_Have_Seen_the_Lord/

Can Words Alone Save?

1. Romans 5:1

2. *All the Last Words of Saints and Sinners*, Herbert Lockyer, Kregel Publications, Grand Rapids, MI, pgs 81, 123, 145

3. John 1:12-13; James 1:18; 1 Corinthians 6:11; Titus 3:5

4. Romans 8:17; Ephesians 1:3

5. 2 Timothy 4:3

6. *Man, The Dwelling Place of God*, A.W. Tozer, WingSpread Publishers, Camp Hill, PA, pg 151

7. *A Shocking Confession from Willow Creek Community Church*, Bob Burney, *October* 30, 2007 http://www.cross-walk.com/pastors/11558438/

8. Author's note: this book can be purchased at http://www.willowcreek.com/wca_prod.asp?invtid=PR30332

9. Romans 10:13-17

The Importance of Sound Doctrine

1. *Time Magazine*, October 9, 2006, "When Not Seeing Is Believing," Andrew Sullivan

2. *The Knowledge of the Holy*, A.W. Tozer, HarperCollins Publishers, pg 4

3. ROMANS, Exposition of chapters 3:20-4:25—Atonement and Justification, pgs 6-7, D. Martyn Lloyd-Jones, The Banner of Truth Trust

4. *The Knowledge of the Holy*, A.W. Tozer, HarperCollins Publishers, pg 89

Who Perverted the Love of God?

1. *The Knowledge of the Holy*, A.W. Tozer, HarperCollins Publishers, pg 4

2. *ROMANS, Exposition of Chapters 2:1-3:20, The Righteous Judgment of God*, D. Martyn Lloyd-Jones, Banner of Truth Publications, pgs 49-50

3. *ROMANS, Exposition of Chapters* 2:1–3:20, *The Righteous Judgment of God*, D. Martyn Lloyd-Jones, Banner of Truth Publications, pgs 56-57

4. Mohler, Albert, www.albertmohler.com, August 28, 2006 blog entry, "The State of Preaching Today" (quoted with permission)

5. Isaiah 5:20

Man-Centered Religion's Definition of a Christian

1. 2 Corinthians 11:4

2. Acts 4:12

The God of Man-Centered Religion

1. *The Knowledge of the Holy*, A.W. Tozer, HarperCollins Publishers, pg 29

2. Exodus 3:14

3. *All the Last Words of Saints and Sinners*, Herbert Lockyer, Kregel Publications, Grand Rapids, MI, pg 156

Works That Deceive and the One Work That Saves

1. *Christianity In Crisis-21st Century*, Hank Hanegraaff, pg 32, Thomas Nelson, Inc.

2. Ephesians 1:19-23

3. Matthew 13:24-30

4. *Christianity In Crisis-21ˢᵗ Century*, Hank Hanegraaff, pg 63, Thomas Nelson, Inc.

5. Ibid, pg xx

6. 2 Corinthians 4:6

7. Galatians 1:6-7

8. *Rock of Ages*

A Real Christian Believes in the Real Jesus

1. *Christianity In Crisis-21ˢᵗ Century*, Hank Hanegraaff, pg 159, Thomas Nelson, Inc.

2. Ibid, pgs 160-162

Can I Know for Certain That I'm Saved?

1. http://en.wikipedia.org/wiki/Council_of_Trent

2. http://www.monergism.com/thethreshold/articles/onsite/counciltrent.html

3. 1 John 1:1-4

4. 1 John 1:5-2:2

5. 1 John 2:3-6, 18-27; 4:1-6

6. 1 Peter 1:23

7. 1 John 2:7-11

8. Colossians 1:24

9. 1 John 2:12-17

10. 1 John 2:28-3:10

11. 1 John 3:11-13

12. 1 John 3:19-24; 5:14-15

13. *The Hope Of His Calling*, A.W. Pink, http://www. pbministries.org/books/pink/Miscellaneous/the_hope_ of_his_calling.htm

God Is Not Like Man, But True Believers Are to Be Like God!

1. *The Knowledge of the Holy*, A.W. Tozer, HarperCollins Publishers, pgs 106-7

2. Ephesians 1:14; 1 Corinthians 6:20

3. Luke 9:23; Romans 12:1-2

4. Galatians 1:6-9

5. *Albert Barnes Commentary*, 2 Corinthians 4:18, SwordSearcher Bible Study Software (www.swordsearcher.com)

The Challenges for Real Christians

1. Hebrews 7:25; 1 Peter 1:23

2. 2 Thessalonians 2:3

3. 1 Corinthians 2:14

4. 1 Corinthians 1:21; 1 Peter 1:23

5. Hebrews 2:10

6. John 5:22

7. Ephesians 4:15

8. *Man, The Dwelling Place of God*, A. W. Tozer, WingSpread Publishers, Camp Hill, PA, pgs 41-45

9. Ephesians 2:8

10. Luke 14:26-27, 33

11. 2 Corinthians 13:5

12. Albert Barnes Commentary, 2 Corinthians 4, SwordSearch Bible Study Software (www.swordsearcher.com)

13. 2 Timothy 3:13

14. Matthew 24:12

15. Matthew 25:6-12

16. Revelation 3:8

17. 2 Thessalonians 2:3

18. 2 Corinthians 5:14

19. 1 Corinthians 3:9-11